F-Notes

Facilitation
for Quality

Kaizen titles from Quality Press

Kaizen Kanban: A Visual Facilitation Approach to Create Prioritized Project Pipelines
Fabrice Bouchereau

Office Kaizen: Transforming Office Operations into a Strategic Competitive Advantage
William Lareau

Modular Kaizen: Continuous and Breakthrough Improvement
Grace L. Duffy

Leadership titles from Quality Press

Culture Is Everything: How to Become a True Culture Warrior and Lead Your Organization to Victory
Jeff Veyera

The Journey: Achieving Sustained Organizational Success
Charles A. Cianfrani, Isaac Sheps, and John E. (Jack) West

Senior Management and Quality: How to Leverage Quality for Profit
Fin Rooney

Problem-solving titles from Quality Press

Root Cause Analysis: The Core of Problem Solving and Corrective Action, Second Edition
Duke Okes

Introduction to 8D Problem Solving
Donald W. Benbow and Ali Zarghami

The Logical Thinking Process: A Systems Approach to Complex Problem Solving
H. William Dettmer

New from Quality Press

Connected, Intelligent, Automated: The Definitive Guide to Digital Transformation and Quality 4.0
N. M. Radziwill

Beyond Compliance Design of a Quality System: Tools and Templates for Integrating Auditing Perspectives
Janet Bautista Smith with Robert Alvarez

The ASQ Certified Quality Improvement Associate Handbook, Fourth Edition
Eds. Grace L. Duffy and Sandra L. Furterer

ISO 56000: Building an Innovation Management System: Bring Creativity and Curiosity to Your QMS
Peter Merrill

For more information on Quality Press titles, please visit our website at: http://www.asq.org/quality-press

F-Notes
Facilitation for Quality

Tracy Owens and
Therese Steiner

First Edition

Quality Press
Milwaukee, Wisconsin

American Society for Quality, Quality Press, Milwaukee 53203
© 2020 by Tracy Owens and Therese Steiner
All rights reserved. Published 2020
Printed in the United States of America

25 24 23 22 21 20   7 6 5 4 3 2 1

Publisher's Cataloging-in-Publication Data
Names: Owens, Tracy Linn, 1967- author. | Steiner, Therese Marie, 1974- author.
Title: F-notes: facilitation for quality / Tracy Owens and Therese Steiner.
Description: Includes bibliographical references and index. | Milwaukee, WI:
Quality Press, 2020.
Identifiers: LCCN: 2020942273 | 978-1-951058-41-8 (pbk.) | 978-1-951058-42-5
(epub) | 978-1-951058-43-2 (pdf)
Subjects: LCSH Group facilitation. | Meetings. | Meetings—Planning. |
Organizational effectiveness—Management. | Total quality management.
| BISAC BUSINESS & ECONOMICS / Project Management | BUSINESS
& ECONOMICS / Decision-Making & Problem Solving | BUSINESS &
ECONOMICS / Quality Control | BUSINESS & ECONOMICS / Total
Quality Management
Classification: LCC HD69.P75 .O924 2020 | DDC 658.4—dc23

Publisher: Seiche Sanders
Managing Editor: Sharon Woodhouse
Sr. Creative Services Specialist: Randy L. Benson

ASQ advances individual, organizational, and community excellence
worldwide through learning, quality improvement, and knowledge exchange.

Bookstores, wholesalers, schools, libraries, businesses, and organizations:
Quality Press books are available at quantity discounts for bulk purchases
for business, trade, or educational uses. For more information, please contact
Quality Press at 800-248-1946 or books@asq.org.

To place orders or browse the selection of all Quality Press titles, visit our
website at: http://www.asq.org/quality-press

∞ Printed on acid-free paper

Quality Press
600 N. Plankinton Ave.
Milwaukee, WI 53203-2914
Email: books@asq.org

ASQ Excellence Through Quality™

Table of Contents

Preface

What Now?

You've been trained in lean, Six Sigma, project management, change management, agile, business process management, or another suite of very useful tools and templates that can really make positive changes possible when used in the right manner and the right sequence. Congratulations! This is a great achievement.

You start your next project by identifying the need, gap, or opportunity, and you draft and agree to a charter. You identify a team of people to help get this initiative started on the right foot and moving in the right direction. You enter the conference room or conference call, and there they are—the project team members are all looking at you to take the lead.

What Now?

We have heard from many friends who are lawyers, doctors, and other professionals that one important thing they do not teach you in law school, medical school, or specialty school is *how to run a business.* This gap is evidenced by the growth of business coaching among specialty practitioners. Managing a law firm or a dental practice is learned from others who have already done it, from affiliate groups who teach each other their best practices, or by trial and error.

The world of process improvement consulting is very similar. Black Belt and Green Belt programs are mainly designed to teach trainees a suite of tools and techniques. Black Belt and Green Belt candidates are shown the tools, instructed on how they are used or completed, given the chance to practice and test them, and minted with a certificate of proficiency. Missing from this progression is the stress of actually deploying a given tool with a group of people—people who are staring at you, the expert, and expecting you to lead them to the land of more efficient and effective work. The process improvement curriculum does not always focus on tools and techniques for effective meeting facilitation.

Missing from certification training is the stress of deploying these tools with real people.

Your certification program may have included a practical component, such as "completion of one project using this body of knowledge," but monitoring, coaching, feedback, and guidance may not have been provided. Or, the certification project may have been done in a controlled environment, closely monitored by a member of the training cadre who was keenly interested in your success. In fact, that person may have been evaluated based on whether your project was successful. The certification process may not have fully prepared you to apply your skills in the "real world" as an expert.

What Now?

As a facilitator, you are in the spotlight from the start of a meeting to its merciful or triumphant conclusion. Everyone is watching you, that is, unless they decide to stop paying attention to you.

Credibility is earned by proving you deserve it. Credibility is lost by failing to demonstrate your expertise.

If that sounds like a lot of pressure, it really is. If you want to frighten yourself from the facilitator role, look up "facilitator losing control of meeting" on YouTube and watch a few examples. When you are facilitating a multihour, sometimes multiday, workshop effort, the pressure is even greater than in a meeting. Let us use the pages of this book to help prepare you to be a successful facilitator.

What You Will Find in This Book

Process improvement should be a constant pursuit in any setting. Nowhere should there be a mindset of "We're doing fine; just leave it all alone and everything will always work fine."

Whether you work in a for-profit business, a government office, a school, a hospital or clinic, a law firm, a not-for-profit organization, your own entrepreneurial entity, or any other type of firm, the pursuit of improvement is going to be important in order to meet your customers' needs in the future.

Whether your own work location is a desk, a store, a cubicle, a truck, a tool room, your home, someone else's home, the basement, the C-suite, or anywhere else, you have the opportunity to make lasting, positive changes for yourself and those around you, including your customers.

In this book, we will share a set of useful techniques to drive such improvements. Our objective is not just to arm you with an expanded menu of tools to use. We want you to have the confidence to deploy them in a live setting with people looking to you for guidance and expertise.

It will be your job to practice and use them, as we cannot be there in the room or on the phone to help you directly. In lieu of hands-on coaching, we offer step-by-step deployment guides for each tool we are sharing.

In our Black Belt training classes, we stress the importance of SIPOC—which is an acronym that traditionally stands for suppliers, inputs, process, outputs, and customers[1]—as a useful tool to get a project started on a solid foundation, and as a technique to orient team members and leaders to the objectives of your work. We demonstrate, often more than once, how to facilitate a group of people in the construction of a good SIPOC. Then it is the trainees' turn to do that job. We invite each of them in turn to build a SIPOC with the help of the team in the room on a topic of our choice. At the moment the first trainee moves to the front of the room to begin this job, we hand that person the SIPOC Construction Guide that is shown in the Appendix. "Follow this word-for-word and step-by-step," we tell them. The process and the results are consistently positive—more positive than they would be without the guide.

---

[1] Look for our revision of SIPOC from Suppliers to Sources in Part 1 of this book.

*The construction guide is a relief; it is a confidence builder,
and it is almost a guarantee of positive results.*

The same is true for all the guides we provide in this book. Clip them, copy them, access them on our website: flexidian.com, and you can even keep this book open to that page while you are preparing and deploying each tool.

The job of a facilitator is to wring every drop of useful information, input, feedback, obstacles, and supporting details from the relevant players in a project or process. The goal of this book is to grow your toolbox and your confidence in doing just that.

Further, it is the job of the facilitator to expedite these improvements. We have found that the techniques described and detailed in these pages enable project leaders to develop and prioritize improvements faster than they would have otherwise.

The Story

By way of example, the story of Kris, our process improvement facilitator, is threaded throughout the book. Kris embarks on several projects with six client organizations and is able to deploy all the tools presented in these chapters. While each tool in the book is presented individually, the story of Kris, the facilitator, helps the reader tie together a sequence of tools to build a success story from start to finish.

The F-Notes

The pages are dotted with facilitator notes, or F-Notes, that are our best tips for achieving success when faced with a group of people. While we surely have not encountered every possible situation that can arise in a workshop or meeting, our experience has prepared us well. We offer F-Notes to help you prevent, handle, adapt to, or mitigate conditions that can lead to the temporary derailment of a meeting or, worse, abandonment of the tool because the group has lost confidence.

We welcome your F-Notes as well! If you have a tip for successful handling of a facilitation pitfall, please send it to us at info@flexidian.com to share with our audience.

Enjoy!

Introduction

How Do We Begin This Journey?

We begin with some true workshop essentials — a few helpful points that should be practiced from the outset of any improvement project.

Workshop Planning

Before a workshop, meeting, training class, kaizen event, or any other project gathering is held, it is critical for the people who have conceived the effort to plan it. The arrival of an invited participant at a meeting that has not been well planned is not only frustrating and unproductive but may also cause future reluctance to participate.

While the scope of this book does not center on creating a project charter, it is a very important document to create at the beginning of a project and prior to conducting a workshop. Charter elements commonly include:

- Background or business case: The narrative reason for embarking on this project

- Problem statement: A quantified description of the current condition, ideally expressing a gap between the current state and the desired state

- Opportunity statement, as an alternative to the problem statement: An expression of how much better our condition could be if we succeed in this project, even if things are already working well

- Objective or goal statement: How much improvement we realistically plan to drive from this specific project

- Project scope: A list of elements in the organization that are included, as well as those excluded from the effort
- Team members: The roles and responsibilities of the full-time project team members, part-time subject-matter resources, project sponsor who breaks down organizational barriers for the team, project leader[2]
- Projected timeline: May include scheduled meetings to review progress with the project sponsor and other stakeholders
- Measures of success: Metrics that will help the team and organization to know how much better conditions are after the project is complete

Documenting these elements helps pave a path for the team's success. Without a charter, a project team is a rowboat crew paddling in all different directions at different rates of speed.

Keep an Eye on the Goal

A quality project, kaizen event, project team meeting, or process improvement workshop often includes an analysis of the current state and a redesign that will lead to an improved future state. It is often the case that the current state includes procedures and practices that may no longer be necessary. Such elements are broken into categories defined as *waste* and are described in texts on lean thinking, in addition to being listed in this book's section on customer journey mapping. The identification of waste is central to process simplification. However, other important elements of the current state must be retained. These are the essential reasons for doing the work, known as critical success factors (CSF), and we describe them in detail at the end of Part 1 in this book. At the beginning of a workshop, we define and post the CSFs for all to see because, in the end, when we have mapped and tested a new, improved work process, we will want to refer back to that list of CSFs to make sure they are all still being honored and executed.

---

[2] More on team roles is shared at the beginning of Part 4 in this book.

Our goals in this book start with instilling confidence in you as a workshop facilitator. But even the word *facilitator* sounds less important than your true role. "Facilitator" makes you sound like someone who watches or guides a discussion and ensures actions are properly recorded. In reality, the success of the workshop depends greatly on your skill in *leading* the participants toward their desired outcomes and selecting useful tools to achieve these results. It can be a high-pressure job. Our objective is to equip you with the tools, techniques, nuances, and responses that will enable you to:

- Make participants feel comfortable and confident in the workshop

- Maintain control of the room

- Handle questions, even questions that could derail the conversation

- Ask probing, relevant questions of the group from your perspective

- Avoid pitfalls

We embark on this journey with a tour of several extremely useful quality tools. Our intent is not to limit the depth of your toolbox but, rather, to highlight these enclosed tools as highly effective in a wide variety of settings. Further, we will reveal many positive techniques for facilitators that we have learned and adapted, and we have the bruises, the shining successes, and the vivid memories of both to share along the way.

Illustration by Miri Owens (@dystopiandreamscaping on Instagram).

1

Identifying and Prioritizing Improvement Opportunities

Quality management begins with the identification of customer needs. That may seem obvious; without a customer to buy the products and services that are being sold, there will be no sales and, therefore, no business. If a customer decides to buy products or services from a particular company, and those products and services fail to provide the expected value, no future purchases from that customer are likely to follow. And when your customers share their negative experiences across social networks, the impact of a single unsatisfied customer expands exponentially.

Quality, then, is about providing value by meeting customer needs.[3] Begin this journey by not only asking your customers, "What is important to you?" but also by building the story of how your product or service helps your customers to achieve their objectives.

A quality professional's depiction of this story is the process map, and there are many varieties. We have found three types to be extremely valuable as basic quality tools:

1. SIPOC is an extremely useful tool, but it is often taught to Green Belts and Black Belts as a "check the box" activity to be completed early in an improvement project and then set aside. We, however, have expanded the SIPOC and emphasize the value it brings. The SIPOC is presented in Part 1 of this book as a foundational tool for successful process improvement initiatives.

2. Customer journey mapping (CJM) reveals the customer's point of view on your product or service. To describe the deployment

---

[3] See Philip Crosby, *Quality is Free: The Art of Making Quality Certain* (New York: Penguin, 1980).

of CJM, we will begin with the popular and useful lean technique of value stream mapping (VSM) and modify the point of view and the details that are needed to ensure the customer's requirements are clear. CJM is also a focus for Part 1.

3. Milestone mapping is an expedient method of capturing essential elements of a specific job during a kaizen workshop. The primary audience for this book is workshop facilitators and project managers, so we will present tools and techniques that bring practical value to you when you are faced with a group of people who are depending on you to bring them positive changes. If you sometimes find yourself leading group discussions on process analysis, then milestone maps will soon add themselves to your growing list of favorite tools. This topic is covered in Part 2.

WHAT IS KAIZEN?

A Japanese word, 改善, which is commonly translated as "change for the better," kaizen typically appears in three forms:

1. The spirit of continuous improvement: looking at your job as a series of experiments and trying to make things simpler all the time.
2. The kaizen event or workshop: bringing the right people together in a room to break apart the current work processes and rebuild them to make them better.
3. A kaizen burst on a process map to highlight an opportunity for improvement.

Here are a few important points about kaizen workshops:

a. Mapping the current state of work is a common and useful first step toward diagnosing opportunities for improvement.
b. Identifying unnecessary work (waste) and causes of defects, delays, and variation are the main goals of the kaizen event.
c. Kaizen events are focused on specific work processes, not on broad, high-level themes.
d. Usually a future-state process map is drawn to illustrate how the work process will be conducted after the workshop.
e. A kaizen event must result in changes; it is not just a session where people meet to complain and generate a wish list.

Facilitator Kris's Journal—Mullins Heating & Cooling: Note 1

I received an email today from Mullins Heating & Cooling[4] requesting assistance in addressing declining revenue concerns. Mullins is a distributor and installer of heating and air conditioning units. The company's management says they have not made any recent changes to their suppliers or processes, yet they have seen a rise in complaints from customers with air conditioning units installed in the last six months. Negative word of mouth is getting out through social media, and they have fewer scheduled installations on the books than ever before. They would like me to come in and work with their team to identify issues and opportunities.

Throughout this book, we include notes from our fictional facilitator, Kris, to provide context of tool application in practice.

My playbook for this project:

1. *SIPOC as a foundational process and scope view. This will help uncover the important variables that might be leading to this downturn.*

2. *"My worst nightmare" innovation game to identify possible failure points*

3. *A basic failure mode and effects analysis (FMEA) to further define and prioritize pain points*

4. *Customer journey mapping to get a clearer picture of the customer's needs and pain points*

5. *Kano analysis to uncover potential hidden opportunities to build customer loyalty*

SIPOC—MORE THAN JUST A LIST OF INPUTS AND OUTPUTS

SIPOC is often taught in quality training as a "check the box" exercise—something to build and then set aside. Black Belt manuals and references give it minimal coverage and usually describe it simply as a way to help everyone see the work from a big-picture

---

[4] All company and individual names have been modified to protect the innocent.

perspective. We yawn at such a description, because it doesn't indicate anything specific that we can do to make our work better. But the SIPOC tool is much more useful than that:

- It is a foundation upon which the remainder of a successful project can be built.

- It is a basis for data analysis to identify root causes of defects, delays, and variation in process outcomes.

- It is a key to scoping additional subprojects that will improve the overall work.

There are two changes we apply to move the SIPOC into prominence and reestablish it as a critical tool for good projects:

1. Redefine the "S" in SIPOC from "suppliers" to "sources."

2. Use the "I" and "O" (inputs and outputs) to identify data for analysis in order to improve.

From "Suppliers" to "Sources"

One challenge with the SIPOC acronym is the presence of the word "suppliers." The roots of lean thinking and Six Sigma lie in manufacturing organizations, and we stand proudly on the shoulders of those who built these successful methodologies. However, the value of this approach to business management has spread far beyond the factory into banks, contact centers, small businesses, nonprofit organizations, schools, hospitals, government agencies, and more. Indeed, this book includes references to the application of quality tools in many of these settings.

The term "supplier" traditionally connotes a vendor bringing raw materials to a factory. This limits the perception of adaptability of the SIPOC.

In a Six Sigma manual, the project leader is instructed to ask:

- Who are your customers? This is the "C" in SIPOC.

- What are the outputs of your process? This is the "O."

- What are your main process steps? This is the "P."

- What are the inputs that are required to do the work? This is the "I."

When you begin to complete the S portion of the SIPOC, the question is typically stated as, "Who are your suppliers?" This is when the eyes of workshop participants glaze over, and they start to think of the SIPOC as purely an academic exercise. What is the purpose of asking who our suppliers are anyway? Are we going to change suppliers of materials based on this diagram? It can seem like a waste of time.

The right question to ask instead is, "What are the sources of each input?" This is broader and more relevant. The use of "sources" instead of "suppliers" increases the applicability of the SIPOC for a wider audience and helps to answer the question about what decisions will be made—you might be able to obtain your inputs from an alternative source. Sources would still include any vendors (suppliers) that might have appeared in the SIPOC using the traditional approach.

Consider:

- One source of an input called "monthly sales statistics" that is used to build a forecast might be the business intelligence query that is drawn on the 10th of each month. Asking for the "supplier" would not resonate with the group, and they might respond with the name of the business intelligence (BI) software package or the vendor company. However, asking for the "source" will start a discussion about the timeliness and accuracy of the BI query.

- One source of an input called "prospect's business information" that is used to qualify a prospective customer in order to pursue a sale might be a web-based questionnaire that the prospect completed on your company's website. The term "supplier" provokes the circular argument that "our customers are also our suppliers" in this context, which minimizes everyone's interest in the SIPOC because it is not telling us anything useful. By asking instead for the "sources" of prospect's business information, the conversation on the usefulness of the web form is opened.

- One source of an input in our facilitator Kris's journal note is the vendor that supplies air conditioning units to the installer, while another source of an input are the homeowners who are buying new units for installation. The vendor would have fit in as a "supplier" in a traditional SIPOC. Broadening the definition of "S" to "sources" includes consideration of the homeowners who contribute new orders and feedback that must be analyzed.

Mind Your I's and O's

Another reason the SIPOC is so often built and then set aside and forgotten is that it doesn't always provide guidance on what to do next. When it is built as a list of five to seven process steps, a handful of outputs, a laundry list of inputs, the obvious customers, and a few vendors under the supplier heading, everyone says, "Oh, that's nice" and quickly forgets about it.

Later in this project you are going to look for the reasons why the work is not being done well today. After you have defined the problem (the "D" in DMAIC), you will collect data to identify the critical variables, the parts of your work that are causing the problem.

DMAIC is an acronym that stands for define, measure, analyze, improve, control; it is a quality-improvement strategy at the heart of Six Sigma.

The frequently asked question becomes, "What data should we collect?" There are two excellent ways to answer that question:

1. Measure all process steps in terms of speed and accuracy.

   a. **Speed.** No matter what work is being done, you can measure how long it takes to complete. Record the start time and the end time. Record the time a request was made to the time it was fulfilled. Do that for the next 20 transactions or the next two weeks' worth of work, and that will help you establish a baseline from which to improve.

   b. **Accuracy.** Once the work is done, record accuracy in one of the following ways:

      i. Was the work done correctly the first time? Measure the proportion or percent of time that no rework or follow-up work was needed.

    ii. Did the work meet the customer's needs exactly as described when the request was made? If yes, add that to the success proportion of section i. above. If not, record the reasons that completeness was not achieved. Next, group those reasons into categories and prepare a pie chart.

    iii. How many times did you have to revise the work before sending it to the customer? These rework loops are often taken as a fact of life, just a part of the way we do business, but they delay final delivery, and they prevent you from doing other value-adding work while you are fixing internal defects.

2. Match inputs to outputs. Look for the relationships between the results of your work and the conditions and factors that come into play before and during the operation. We will go so far as to say that the ability to match inputs to outputs in your work is tantamount to predicting the future. Would you like to be able to predict the future?

Facilitator Kris's Journal—Mullins Heating & Cooling: Note 2

Today was Day 1 at the Mullins Heating & Cooling office. I was pleased to discover they keep detailed records of every installation. With these data, I can help them learn what problems need to be addressed and prevented on future installations. The data comprise the inputs and outputs of their process. The SIPOC will be a critical tool on this project. By matching the inputs to the outputs of specific installation instances, we can show which inputs are most likely to result in successful outcomes.

SIPOC IN PRACTICE

We have facilitated hundreds of groups through the successful construction of a useful SIPOC, and, in most cases, we have simulated SIPOC creation with an example before moving into mapping the actual work being done with the group in the room with us. A common example we have used is growing tomatoes:

"Who in this room has ever grown tomatoes?" we ask. The number of people who acknowledge having grown tomatoes at home is surprisingly high in most groups.

"What are the main elements of growing tomatoes?" we ask. The answers are as plentiful as slugs in a vegetable garden:

Water them	Time for growing
Stakes	Cages around the plants
Fertilizer	Good soil
Sunlight	Rabbits and deer
Good seeds	Shoots instead of seeds

We summarize those comments and write in the center of the whiteboard (see Figure 1.1):

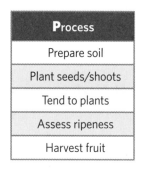

Figure 1.1 Process column in a new SIPOC that is under construction.

Ask the group, "Does that look right? I realize there are a lot more things to do, but is this a good high-level summary?" They usually agree.

It is advisable to proceed to the right side of the diagram next with outputs and customers and then to the left with inputs and sources, so the group is thinking of the ultimate results of the work while discussing the factors that go into producing it (see critical success factors below). If your situation suggests a need to go left then right, as the facilitator, you are free to take it in that direction.

F-Note: We usually begin with the "P" column (process) when the process improvement target is work that is already being done today and needs to get better. When building a SIPOC with a group of people who intend to construct a new product or service, it is not a bad idea to begin with the "O" column (outputs) to identify the things you intend to deliver. Some groups will find it advantageous to begin with the "C" column (customers), because customer identification is not always perfectly clear and can change from time to time.

We then ask the group, "What are the results of the growing-tomatoes process?" *This is a very important moment! You must not let the only answer to this question be "tomatoes!"*

In fact, it is useful to be very deliberate in stating, "Most groups stop by saying 'tomatoes' and leave it at that. This is not enough." If you are mapping the process for generating a report and you list under the outputs column only "the report"; or if you are mapping a sales cycle and your only entry under outputs is "close the sale"; or if you are building a SIPOC for recruiting a new staff member and the only output listed is "new hire," the team is limited in the ability to answer the question, "How do we know we did a good job?"

Tell the group that they must continue the outputs section of the SIPOC by listing the measurable characteristics of the tomatoes in order to answer that question after every harvest.

F-Note: The SIPOC helps the group answer the question, "How do we know we did a good job?"

"What are the measurable characteristics of your tomato crop?" we ask.

Typical responses include:

Taste	Color	Quantity	Quality
Size	Juiciness	Firmness	

Another important question under outputs is, "What are the *undesirable* results of this work?" If we only track the positive results, we are ignoring on the SIPOC the defects that we are trying to prevent. This exercise will be fruitless, so to speak. When prompted with this question, the group calls out, "Rotten tomatoes!" And when asked how that is measured, they answer with either the total number of failed tomatoes or the proportion of the total crop that is unsuitable for delivery. Does this sound overly analytical for a discussion about homegrown tomatoes? Yes, and that means we are getting close to the time to introduce SIPOC construction for a job the assembled group really does care about.

The customer section answers the question, "Who is the customer of each output?" Sometimes there are multiple customers, some external to the organization and some internal. Don't leave anybody off the chart, but also don't add customers if there is no corresponding output. "Every output has a customer" is your reminder to the group when completing the customer section.

Move now to the left for the inputs section. This is easy: just look at each of the items under process and ask, one-by-one, "What do you need in order to complete process step #1?" Continue asking, "What else?" until no further responses are offered, and then move to the next step and ask the same question.

Next, there should be a source for each input. The final result is a SIPOC like the one in Table 1.1.

Now you are at the point where the most important reason for building a SIPOC can be revealed. Ask the tomato growers in the room, "Did you ever have an especially great harvest?" Heads will nod affirmation. Then immediately ask, "Did you ever have a crop that was particularly woeful or sad?" Again, they will agree that, yes, this has happened to them.

And now here is your statement of SIPOC importance:

The greatest crop you ever produced (pointing to the outputs column), as measured by these characteristics, was a result of the inputs you used to grow those tomatoes. And if you can identify the variables (pointing to the inputs column) that led to success in that crop, you can reproduce that combination and have similar success.

The worst crop that grew in your yard (pointing again to outputs), as measured by these details, was also a result of these inputs. If you can isolate the factors that led to failure, you can eliminate them, minimize them, or mitigate their impact to reduce failure in the future.

Matching inputs to outputs enables you to predict the future and improve your chances of success.

Sources	Inputs	Process	Outputs	Customers
Pot or yard	Soil (pH, minerals)	Prepare soil	Ripe tomatoes	Family
Stores	Seeds (number, type)	Plant seeds/ shoots	Size (circumference, weight)	(to eat)
Distilled or tap	Water (how much)	Tend the plants	Color (scale green to red)	
	Water (how often)		Quantity (count)	
Vendor	Fertilizer (25-10-15?)		Taste (subjective)	
	Support (stake, cage)		Firmness (thumbprint)	
	Color scale	Assess ripeness	Soft tomatoes	Sauce
	Basket	Harvest the fruit	Rotten tomatoes	Discarded

Table 1.1 Completed SIPOC for growing tomatoes.

Rows and Columns

If you can organize all your transactions, all your jobs, your customer's full life cycle with all touchpoints, all the calls your team has taken — in short, all the work you do — into rows and columns of data, you can study your process at levels of detail not previously possible. Every row is one transaction. Every column is a factor or detail about that transaction.

F-Note:
- *Outputs do not have to be itemized for each process step; they can be the collective results of the overall process.*
- *There is a customer for each output.*
- *Inputs, however, are itemized. List the inputs required to complete each process step.*
- *There should be a source for each input.*

Facilitator Kris's Journal—Mullins Heating & Cooling: Note 3

Today was Day 2 at the Mullins Heating & Cooling office. I facilitated a SIPOC session with the team. We then studied their installation records for the data aligned to the inputs and outputs from the SIPOC (see data excerpt in Table 1.2):

Customer	Product	Day	Time	Rain?	Home	Pre-paid?	Inst. time	Call back?
1252	AV-1	FRI	8 a.m.	Yes	Two-story	Y	2.5	Y
1442	AV-2	FRI	1 p.m.	No	One-story	N	2.75	N
2811	AV-2	THU	2 p.m.	No	Two-story	Y	1.45	N
2932	AV-3	THU	9 a.m.	No	One-story	Y	1.45	Y

Table 1.2 Extract of installer's data collection record.

We determined that the measures of success for an installation are: 1) how long it takes (speed); and 2) whether the installer was called back after the installation to make an adjustment or correction (accuracy). These are the two rightmost columns. All the other columns are variables or conditions of the installation. They can use this data table to study what conditions cause longer installations and callbacks.

This is a very small sample, but at a glance we noted that installations seem to take longer on Fridays than they do on Thursdays, and morning installations lead to callbacks more than afternoon jobs. If a larger, more thorough data study[5] leads to these same conclusions, then Mullins will have a factual basis to take action. My recommendation to them for the next steps will be to identify the reasons for callbacks on morning installations and also to observe the team to learn why Friday installations consume more time than Thursday jobs.

Building the SIPOC with the project team was an eye-opening exercise, an early source of alignment among team members, and the basis for next-step data collection and analysis. I am glad I didn't overlook the importance of the SIPOC early in this project.

---

[5] A study using statistical analysis techniques like regression, analysis of variance, and t-tests, is beyond the scope of this book.

In tomorrow's workshop with the project team, I'll introduce a tool known as "my worst nightmare."

MY WORST NIGHTMARE—APPLYING INNOVATION GAMES TO FAILURE IDENTIFICATION

The first of two innovation games we highlight in this book that were popularized by Luke Hohmann,[6] my worst nightmare (MWN) is a great way to identify possible failures in your product or service.

As described by Hohmann, the game is played by presenting a group with a specific situation to evaluate. This is usually your company's product or service. The facilitator asks the group members to illustrate their worst nightmare associated with a specific element of their products or services on a whiteboard, flipchart, or shared virtual workspace.

F-Note: If you are working virtually rather than with a colocated group, prepare a shared workspace in advance. Many conferencing tools, such as Microsoft Teams, WebEx, and Zoom, include a virtual whiteboard that can be handy for this purpose.

"Worst nightmare" is obviously a very subjective response, so there can be a lot of variation in the drawings that will be produced.

Our approach is a bit different in that we do not ask for illustrations. Artwork is certainly welcome but not required. We ask everyone to write brief descriptions or bullet points using sticky notes on the topic of what are the worst possible outcomes of this work. As we will highlight a few times in this book, anonymity should be preserved by facilitators, allowing those who contribute ideas to reveal themselves only if and when they are ready. We then collect the sticky notes from all the participants and affix them to the flipchart or smooth wall ourselves.

It is helpful to demonstrate the MWN concept prior to actually beginning the exercise on the topic at hand. We like to use the drive-through coffee shop as a working example (see Figure 1.2). Here's how it works: Ask the group, "What is your worst nightmare when

---

[6] Luke Hohmann, *Innovation Games* (New York: Addison Wesley, 2007).

driving through the coffee shop in the morning?" and ask them to answer out loud. When you get answers like the coffee is cold, the pastry is stale, and the cashier is impolite, you might playfully suggest that, if those are really the *worst* things that can happen, the coffee shop has no hope of ever fully pleasing you and should prepare for a mountain of complaints. Ask them then to stretch and really think of nightmare scenarios. There may be some chuckling when someone contributes *nuclear winter* as a response, but at least you have them thinking!

My Worst Nightmare—The Coffee Shop

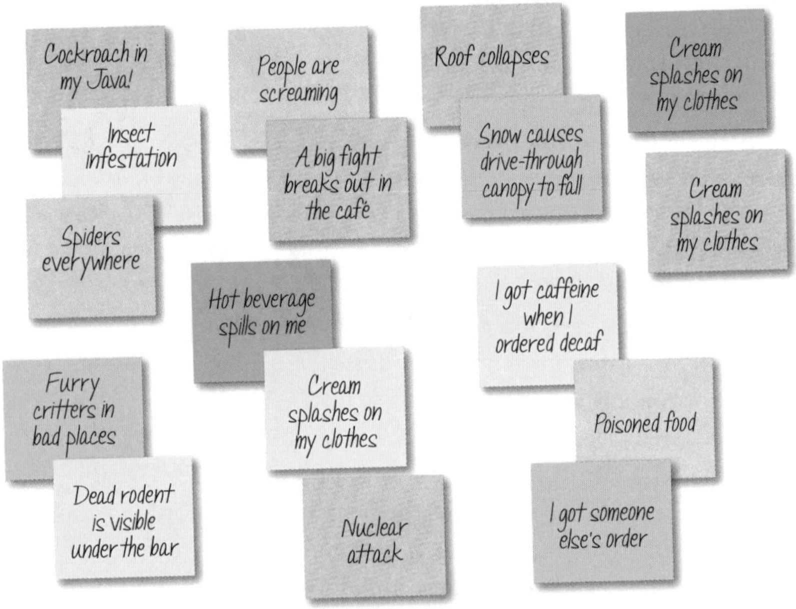

Figure 1.2 Sample My Worst Nightmare (MWN) output.

The importance of MWN is to reveal potential failures to meet your customer's needs. In addition to being a thought-starter, the results of MWN can actually feed the FMEA (the next topic in this book) that you are building in your project.

If you have a negative current among the participants, then MWN is the game for you.

F-Note: Use MWN to engage stakeholders who are resistant to the change effort. The device of the game allows naysayers to express their concerns in a safe and constructive context. The debrief questions then involve these same people in thinking about how to mitigate their concerns.

When you ask the question, "What can possibly go wrong with [our product, our service, our delivery, our sales cycle, our software, our project management, our course offerings, our city event, or anything else you are studying]?" even the most unpleasant or critical comment is welcome because *that is the name of the game.* Dutifully collect all sticky notes and place them impartially on a vertical workspace.

Your role as the facilitator in MWN now kicks into a higher gear. Make sure every item that was written is read out loud for all to hear. You don't have to be the one who reads them, though you usually are; this job can be delegated. Once the items have been read out loud, ask the group a series of debrief questions:

F-Note: A simple approach to collecting MWN inputs virtually is to have participants email, text, or chat them to you. As each note arrives, copy/paste the comment anonymously into a document that you can then screen share to the team.

- Which ideas surprised you?
- What images did these ideas conjure in your mind?
- Which of them are more likely to actually happen than others?
- What can we do to prevent them?

Naturally, this is our objective—to generate a list of potential problems that need to be prevented.

F-Note: The MWN game can also be useful as a separate exercise to start the creativity flowing in a group before you begin the main part of your meeting. Use the coffee shop or another situation that most everyone has likely experienced.

Facilitator Kris's Journal—Mullins Heating & Cooling: Note 4

Day 3 at the Mullins office, the morning: We played MWN, and it really got the team thinking. The team started out with scenarios of earthquakes and hurricanes preventing installations. I then asked them to put themselves into their customers' shoes: What do you think your customers' worst nightmares are? What happens when the air conditioner installation goes poorly? This led to different responses:

- An increase in humidity caused by faulty air conditioning, which causes all the paint to peel off the homeowner's walls

- An electrical short that causes the home to fill with smoke

- No air conditioning on the hottest days of the year

- An air handler admitting cockroaches or spiders into the home's air ducts

Yikes, what a nightmare!

After generating the list of both plausible and implausible nightmare scenarios, I will move the team this afternoon right into building an FMEA to assess the risk levels and prioritize problems they should anticipate and address.

FLEX FMEA—A LESS COMPLEX
APPROACH TO PRIORITIZING ACTIONS

The failure mode and effects analysis (FMEA) is an important quality tool with a long history that started in the U.S. military service in the late 1940s.[7] Like any good risk-analysis tool, it captures and quantifies both the likelihood of specific types of problems and the severity of each. The FMEA label for "likelihood" is OCC, meaning frequency of occurrence. This is a measure of how often a problem happens or how likely it would be to happen for a process or product not yet in service. Severity is abbreviated SEV on an FMEA and is a measure of how serious the problem is whenever it does happen (see Figure 1.3).

Severity					
Likelihood	1	2	3	4	5
5					
4					
3					
2					
1					

Figure 1.3 A typical risk analysis includes likelihood of the problem and severity of the problem.

An added strength of the FMEA is a feature that is not found in typical risk-analysis tools. It is the detection score (DET), which is a measure of how quickly or easily the problem is identified.

There are a few challenges in building an FMEA, so it is not always embraced by those in an office setting. Difficulties include:

1. The chart itself is quite a large document, which causes trepidation when shown to a group of people, especially when accompanied by the phrase, "OK, we're going to fill this out now."

2. Haggling over scoring, such as whether a specific failure is a 6 in severity or a 7, can be a tedious exercise. A remedy for this is to use the 1, 3, and 9 scales shown in Table 1.3, which leads to a more succinct and healthy debate.

---

[7] MIL-P-1629, Procedures for Performing FMEA (January, 1960).

3. Listing all possible failures is a daunting task. Some people in the room will prefer to keep the discussion only on those failures that are most common or most recent, while others will bring up very infrequent possible problems in the spirit of building an exhaustive list.

4. The FMEA is a two-part process: you complete the analysis of the current state now to identify and prioritize problems, and then you complete the FMEA again later after improvements have been made and rescore it. Revisiting the FMEA is usually about as unappetizing as bringing it up in the first place.

SEV (severity of the problem)		OCC (frequency or likelihood of occurrence)		DET (ease of detection)	
10	Loss of life	10	Always	10	Cannot detect
9	Critical	9	1 in 10	9	Defect reaches customer
8		8		8	
7	> $100,000	7	1 in 100	7	20% likely to detect
6		6		6	
5		5		5	
4		4		4	
3	Major / > $1,000	3	1 in 1,000 / Sometimes	3	50% likely to detect / catch internally
2	Minor	2			
1	Nuisance	1	1 in 10,000/ Rarely	1	95% likely to detect / instantly found

Table 1.3 Common scoring for FMEA.

Our approach simplifies the preparation of an FMEA and still promotes objective prioritization of problems to be addressed. We build on the MWN game and the SIPOC we've constructed. While we will still score each potential failure according to its frequency or likelihood of occurrence, its severity, and its detectability, we will simplify the form. Then those three numerical scores are multiplied together to produce the risk prioritization number (RPN), and the RPNs for individual failures can be ranked from highest to lowest. This gives the team an order of priority for action.

F-Note: When a group has developed a list of problems or actions and needs to decide how to prioritize them, it can be difficult to settle on a method for making that decision. Often the loudest voice or the highest-ranking person commands the team's priorities, but that may not always be the best way to decide. Popular techniques include voting and sorting based on each item's projected impact and effort. In this book, we are proposing two team-based methods for prioritization: the FMEA shown here, and the clock diagram described in Part 2. These tools can make prioritization decisions more objective.

Facilitator Kris's Journal—Mullins Heating & Cooling: Note 5

Day 3 continued at the Mullins office, the afternoon: When I reviewed the Mullins installation records yesterday evening (after Day 2 with the team), I extracted a list of the reported issues that I could find in the records and put these into a column in a simple spreadsheet. Based on the SIPOC exercise, I added a few more issues that were mentioned when discussing negative outputs. After the MWN exercise this morning, while the team took a lunch break, I added the ideas generated in MWN to this same column, creating what seemed like a rather daunting list of potential issues.

F-Note: Save time for the team by preparing forms and tools in advance or on breaks, even if it means you have less time to eat!

With the potential issues in the first column, I added three more headings on the sheet like so:

Potential issue	If it happens, how severe is the impact to the customer? [SEV]	How likely is this to occur or how often has it occurred? [OCC]	How easy is it to detect this issue before it impacts the customer? [DET]

When the team reconvened from the lunch break, we first reviewed the list of potential issues, adding a couple more based on the team's thoughts in going through the list.

For each item, we then completed the worksheet, spending no more than a few minutes on each row.

In the SEV column, we rated the items using the scale:

> *10 = Loss of the structure (meaning this issue would destroy the customer's home)*
>
> *9 = Critical impact to the customer*
>
> *3 = Major impact to the customer*
>
> *1 = Minor impact or nuisance*

In the OCC column, we rated the items using the scale:

> *9 = This issue is likely to occur on almost every installation*
>
> *7 = This issue occurs very frequently*
>
> *3 = This issue occurs sometimes*
>
> *1 = This issue rarely occurs or is not at all likely*

In the DET column, we rated the items using the scale:

> *9 = We only find out about this issue if the customer reports it to us*
>
> *3 = About half the time we catch this issue before the customer reports it to us*
>
> *1 = We know about this issue before the customer is impacted in any way*

By keeping the scales numerically separated and clearly defined, we were able to quickly rate each item without a lot of disagreement over specific numbers. I then added a column with the formula SEV x OCC x DET and sorted the result in descending order. This resulted in a ranked list with the issues that are most severe, most likely to occur, and most likely to reach the customer without internal detection rising to the top of the list (see Table 1.4).

Potential issue	[SEV]	[OCC]	[DET]	[RPN]	Prevention measures
Initial settings not preferred	1	7	3	21	
Spare air filters not provided	1	3	3	9	
Thermostat not calibrated	3	3	9	81	
Electricity not reset	9	1	3	27	
Equipment not grounded	10	1	9	90	
Outside pipes not covered	3	9	1	27	
Area not cleaned	1	1	3	3	

Table 1.4 Sample unsorted FMEA for Mullins Heating & Cooling.

With this prioritized list of potential issues, we're getting close to starting some action planning. However, it's important to first validate our thinking through voice of the customer (VoC) data, if possible. I asked the team to think about how they might get some more direct feedback from customers before we reconvene our work next week.

F-Note: If there is a tie between two or more RPNs, use the SEV score to rank the relative importance.

Flex FMEA Modification

In addition to the four challenges in building an FMEA that are listed previously, the scoring factors used in the FMEA are not always clearly understood. Each one presents some difficulty in explaining the value it brings.

Frequency of occurrence may be the simplest, but even this factor can be hard to grasp. If the problems the team is discussing are already being experienced, and there is a recorded history of how often each has been presented, then it is easy to recall and assess how often each problem is occurring. But, if the discussion centers on potential problems, or the team is talking about a future state with problems that have not yet begun, then the OCC category can be used to evaluate the likelihood of each problem.

Severity most commonly refers to the impact each problem will have on the customer, as shown previously in Facilitator Kris's journal. It is possible, however, to turn the focus of the SEV score inward and evaluate the ease of resolving the issue instead. In this case, the scoring would look like this:

1 = Fast or immediate resolution

3 = 10-15 minutes to resolve (Your team can decide what range of time to use.)

9 = Derails my productivity to resolve this issue OR >30 minutes to resolve

The idea of detection is not always clear nor is it always easy to explain. In a service setting, the detection of a problem often depends on the customer's notification via an inbound call or email, so score would already be a 9 based on the scale shown above. Instead of using the traditional DET score, the flex FMEA changes this value to DIG for "diagnosis." Evaluate how easy it is to diagnose the problem in the first place. It is common for a caller, or even a fellow employee, to believe that one problem is occurring when in fact that is not the true issue. The observed condition may be a symptom of a larger problem. Uncovering the root cause is important if true problem solving and process improvement are going to be successful.

Given these modifications to traditional FMEA, the flex FMEA scoring can look like Table 1.5.

SEV (severity of the problem or ease of resolution)		OCC (frequency or likelihood of occurrence)		DET/DIG (how easily the problem is detected or diagnosed)	
9	Critical loss for customer, OR more than 30 minutes to resolve	9	Always, daily, or multiple times per day, OR highly likely to occur	9	Not detected until it reaches the customer, OR original problem expressed is not the real problem
3	Major loss for customer, OR 10–15 minutes to resolve	3	Sometimes, not chronic, OR likely to occur	3	Detected later, but before it reaches the customer, OR several questions are needed to uncover the true problem
1	Minor loss for customer, OR nuisance, fast resolution	1	Rare, infrequent, OR not likely to occur often	1	Detected immediately, OR diagnosed immediately

Table 1.5 Flex FMEA scoring.

F-Note: Try to make the FMEA a conversation instead of an exercise in filling the blanks on the form. It may be best to not even show the table to the group while discussing it. For each problem that is raised, ask the group:

- How serious is this problem? (SEV score)
- How often does it occur? (OCC score)
- How easy is it to uncover the real root cause? (DET/DIG score)

Add the numerical values to the FMEA after the discussion. Show the completed table to the team and let them verify that you have captured the scoring correctly. Then congratulate them for creating such a valuable worksheet!

Facilitator Kris's Journal—Mullins Heating & Cooling: Note 6

Day 4 at Mullins office: voice of the customer

*The Mullins team is now ready to look at things from their customers'
perspectives, and they have been brave enough to invite some of their
complaining customers into the office to better understand what happened.
I always recommend getting the VoC as directly as possible, so this is
great. Here is one of the stories they heard from the visiting customers:*

> *One young, newly married couple explained they recently moved into
> a home they had just purchased. The two-story house was 35 years old
> with a fenced yard and clean windows that seemed to do a good job of
> keeping the cool air inside during this very warm summer. Furniture
> fit neatly in all the rooms, and the couple was excited to start a new
> family life.*
>
> *Prior to closing the sale, the home inspector approved the structure. The
> inspection seemed like just a formality; but three weeks after moving in,
> the couple experienced an untimely problem: the air conditioner was not
> working properly. The hot weather was not quite the housewarming
> they had in mind!*
>
> *Naturally, their first phone call was to the number printed on the
> sticker affixed to the air conditioning unit—Mullins Heating &
> Cooling, the company that had performed the installation. The cheerful
> voice at the other end of the phone confirmed the couple was within the
> warranty period and stated that "we can have a technician visit you the
> day after tomorrow sometime between 8 a.m. and noon."*
>
> *Two more days and four hours later, the technician's visit was
> inconclusive. A second visit revealed a manufacturing defect with the
> unit. Mullins indicated they would have to contact their factory
> supplier representative for a second opinion. Meanwhile, the
> temperature of the house and its occupants continued to rise. By now,
> they were ranting about Mullins on social media and to any friend and
> neighbor within earshot.*

*After the customers left the office, the Mullins team was somewhat
deflated and defensive. "Most of these customer complaints aren't even
our fault—manufacturer's defects are our supplier's fault!"*

I closed out the day reminding them that this gift of feedback is better received than ignored — we can't improve if we aren't ready to tackle the tough issues. Tomorrow we will start working on customer journey maps to see how well our work aligns with our customers' expectations.

CUSTOMER JOURNEY MAPPING—
UNDERSTANDING THE GEMBA OF THE CUSTOMER

The next in our series of valuable tools is the customer journey map (CJM). To introduce the CJM, though, we begin by referring to the time-honored lean technique of value stream mapping (VSM). We use VSMs to represent our processes visually, often mapping out the current state by taking a gemba walk. Gemba is a Japanese word that means the "real place," adapted for quality management to mean "the place where the work is done." Gemba for process mapping means walking the job from start to finish to experience it as closely as possible to reality. We walk the factory floor or otherwise follow the work, documenting it along the way.

Visualizing the work process and mapping the value stream are useful techniques to analyze internal jobs to optimize the capability of delivering output that is aligned with our customer's requirements on the first pass.

VSM

VSM is a popular and useful lean technique for visualizing a work process and studying it for improvement opportunities. Most commonly used in manufacturing and supply chain settings, a VSM begins its life as a list of tasks, each of which is measured in terms of its:

- Speed (cycle time for each step and overall lead time from request to fulfillment)
- Accuracy (defect and rework rates associated with each step)
- Required resources (personnel, materials, inventory, and tools needed)
- Productivity (value-adding time, changeover time, and uptime)

Unlike a typical flowchart, the VSM shows these and other bits of useful data in data boxes on the map. Also depicted are the information flows between suppliers, customers, and the production facility. In all, the VSM is a very comprehensive picture of the work being done today, and it can be redrawn after improvements are identified to show the future state.

In VSM exercises, the customer is represented by a single shape:

But our customers are more than the bundle of their functional requirements. While we may satisfy our customers by meeting functional requirements on time and within budget, so can our competitors. Moving customers from *satisfied* to *loyal*, as shown in the hierarchy in Figure 1.4, necessitates connecting with them on a deeper level.

Create **evangelists/promoters** by meeting unrecognized needs and making emotional connections.

Create **loyalty** among your customers by meeting desires and anticipating needs.

Create **satisfaction** by meeting expectations and functional requirements.

Figure 1.4 Simplified customer hierarchy.

We need to start listening to our customers' stories and understanding the journey they take with us to build and sustain loyal relationships. By introducing elements of CJM into your continuous improvement workshops, you can start to connect with your customers on a deeper, more personal level.

CJM involves identifying with your customers as fully actualized human beings who have needs that go beyond functional requirements. Take that single symbol from the VSM and expand it to the full customer experience. The customer's gemba is not on our factory floor. To map the customer's journey, it is important to view your work from your customer's point of view. You can do this by listening to your customers' stories.

You can consult countless books and websites about CJM to learn the "textbook" process. The basic elements include: (1) customer personas or profiles; (2) a timeline or set of life-cycle stages; (3) steps the customer takes, which may be referred to as touchpoints; (4) customer's thoughts, perceptions, or feelings at the touchpoints; (5) identification of highlights and pain points, and (6) supporting evidence. We like to add two elements from lean in our approach to journey mapping: kaizen bursts and identification of wastes.

Fundamentally, the journey map is a method to visualize and analyze the end-to-end experience of the customer throughout his or her relationship with your product, services, or company.

THERESE'S STORY

When my husband and I moved into our new home, we contacted the home security company listed on the wall panel and signed a service contract. For years, we were satisfied customers. Then we decided to upgrade the system to a wireless setup. We contacted our service provider. After several contact attempts, a representative at last came to our house, and we discussed options. She left an offer with us, indicating it was good for 10 days. When we tried to contact her again, she was out of the office with no apparent backup. By the time she returned, the 10-day window was closed, and their process required a new estimate based on a new home visit.

Fed up, we contacted a competitor. The competitor was consistently responsive and easy to work with throughout the experience.

The two providers used the same software. Their service offerings were virtually identical. The competitor's costs were slightly higher than the original provider. On paper, both met our functional requirements, and the original provider only won on cost. We signed quickly with the competitor because its service was superior, and we have not looked back. –T.S.

We all have stories like this. How do you listen to your customers' stories?

Typically, the first step in journey mapping is understanding the different customer profiles, or personas, that represent your current or *desired* customer base. A customer persona is more than just a segment of your market. It helps to give the persona a name, a picture, and the personality of a fictitious customer. Your persona is "inspired by the true story" of your customer to make him or her as realistic as possible while still being suitably representational.

SOME CUSTOMER JOURNEY TERMINOLOGY

Persona = a representation of your customer based on existing customer data or market research about your prospective customers

Customer life cycle = stages a customer goes through during their relationship with your company. Labels vary, but conceptually it includes initial awareness, purchase, using the product/service, and deciding whether to renew/repurchase

Touchpoint = any interaction a customer has with your products, services, website/app, or people

Moment of truth = a critical point in the customer journey that is likely to make or break the experience for the customer

After defining the customer persona, we map the experience of the customer across the life cycle, we identify pain points as well as strengths, and then we identify and prioritize improvements to address these opportunities.

It's best not to map your customer journey by yourself. This should be a team effort, ideally with a cross-functional team of people who work in different stages of the customer life cycle.

F-Note: While the persona is a useful device, for the purposes of an efficient process improvement workshop, you may consider instead using basic, general key characteristics of an average customer.

Before the CJM Workshop: Scope Identification

Identify the *problem statement* and the *objective* of your workshop, which are two key elements of a project charter. For this we will use the following example:

Problem statement: Customer renewals of our home security services have declined by 20% over the last five years. New sales are not making up for this decline in renewals, so overall revenue is down. We need to more fully understand and address what is driving customer attrition.

Objective: The goal of this workshop is to identify the root causes of this decline and prioritize actions to remediate. The output will include: (1) a CJM; (2) agreed-upon and prioritized opportunities for improvement; and (3) an action plan with owners and timeline assigned (see Part 4 for more on action registers).

As the facilitator, be sure you have clear agreement with the workshop sponsor and key stakeholders on the problem statement and objective. It is critical that you are aligned on the desired result of the workshop in order to deliver success. It is also important that the sponsor and stakeholders understand that this workshop is a starting point and that work will be needed following the workshop to deliver the desired improvements.

F-Note: Consider documenting the outline of the customer journey, including the life-cycle stages and the major touchpoints, based on customer stories and through interviews with internals who interact with customers, prior to the workshop. While this can be done within the workshop itself, creating an outline of the journey as prework helps focus the workshop attendees and move things along more quickly. If you do gather information in advance as prework, be sure to leverage the prework in the workshop and don't have attendees repeat what has already been gathered.

Gather your customer stories. Get as much information about the problem statement as you can from the customer's perspective. Sources of customer stories include survey data, inquiries into your customer service or help desk, feedback entries, social media postings, sales interactions, etc. These VoC sources become your "gemba walk" of the customer experience.

Identify the critical workshop attendees. Work with your sponsor and key stakeholders to ensure all departments and functions that impact a customer's experience within the scope of your problem statement are represented in the workshop. Ensure you have individuals with direct knowledge of related processes and customer experiences and also individuals with decision authority to make relevant changes as participants.

F-Note: By bringing the disparate functions of your organization together in a CJM workshop, as attendees hear each other's perspective and place in the customer journey, often for the first time, there are likely to be many "aha" moments. This increased visibility across silos of an organization is one of the values of a CJM workshop.

Based on the customer stories you gathered prior to the workshop, create representative customers or personas. Review these with your workshop sponsor for alignment as well. Consider sending the personas to participants in advance, giving them an opportunity to review and suggest edits so the workshop team is aligned on personas ahead of the workshop.

Examples of personas for our problem statement may include:

PERSONA: SALLY HOMEOWNER

Sally is a 40-something woman living in suburban middle America. She works full time Monday through Friday and has a 40-minute commute to and from the office each day.

She works in a job that would be challenging to perform remotely from home. When she is home, Sally takes care of her two toddlers. She doesn't have much flexibility during the work week for home visits; her time is very valuable to her. Since she is away from home frequently, she needs to feel that her home is safe and not a likely target for crime. Sally no longer has a landline in her home, so she needs her security system to be wireless.

PERSONA: BRUCE RETIREE

 Bruce is 82 and living alone in his apartment in the city. He lives on the first floor because stairs are difficult for him. But he is always concerned that his first-floor location makes him more vulnerable to home break-ins.

Bruce is home most of the time but is slow to answer the door and nervous about strangers. Bruce would like to be able to see who is at the door before he answers it and without getting up from his chair.

The personas should represent your target customers, their needs, and their concerns, based on the scope of your workshop and the research you have done using your VoC data. The personas serve a couple of purposes: (1) keeping the customer "real" and front of mind; and (2) ensuring agreed-upon improvements align to the customers' needs.

Workshop Preparation

Lay out a framework for your journey map visualization in advance so you can focus on the journey elements and customer pain points during the workshop.

STEP 1: BUILD CUSTOMER PERSONAS

Take some time to select key personas that are most representative of your target customers and most likely to drive discussion in the workshop. These may be, for example, the personas representing the largest percentages of your customer base, highest revenue, or greatest risk. We suggest tackling no more than two to three personas within a workshop in order to maintain engagement and minimize confusion. You may even want to focus on just one persona, as long as that one will enable you to achieve the objectives of your workshop.

For each selected persona, create a journey mapping work area. This may be a separate file or worksheet if you are mapping digitally, or it may be separate flip charts, whiteboards, etc. We find it useful to summarize the customer persona for each map on the side of the map page itself or somewhere in your workspace so the customer is front of mind throughout the workshop. To save time, set up your journey pages in advance of the workshop. See Figure 1.5 for an example.

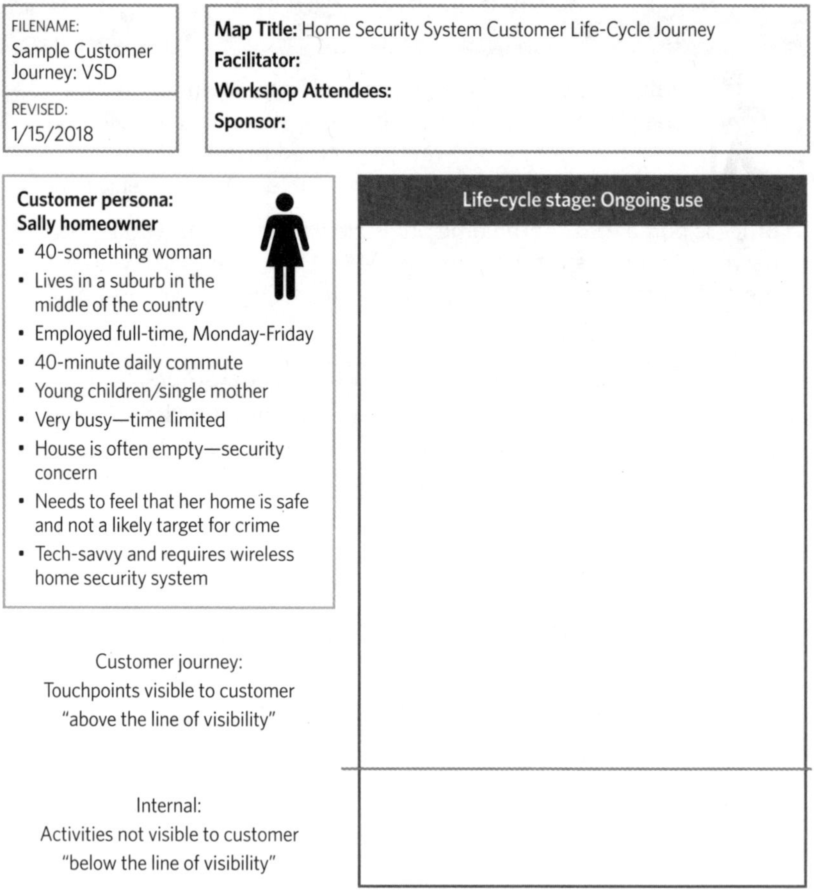

FILENAME: Sample Customer Journey: VSD	Map Title: Home Security System Customer Life-Cycle Journey
	Facilitator:
REVISED: 1/15/2018	Workshop Attendees: Sponsor:

Customer persona:
Sally homeowner

- 40-something woman
- Lives in a suburb in the middle of the country
- Employed full-time, Monday-Friday
- 40-minute daily commute
- Young children/single mother
- Very busy—time limited
- House is often empty—security concern
- Needs to feel that her home is safe and not a likely target for crime
- Tech-savvy and requires wireless home security system

Life-cycle stage: Ongoing use

Customer journey:
Touchpoints visible to customer
"above the line of visibility"

Internal:
Activities not visible to customer
"below the line of visibility"

Figure 1.5 Customer journey map (CJM) worksheet created in Visio with eVSM[8] add-on.

STEP 2: ESTABLISH LIFE-CYCLE STAGES

The customer's life cycle with your product or service begins when they first become aware of a need and start to pursue options to meet that need. It continues through purchase and use, ending with termination or looping around again to repurchase, renewal, or upsell. Depending on scope, you may need to map the full life cycle or just selected segments of the journey. In our example, since

[8] eVSM Group, Mason, Ohio, http://www.evsm.com

we are focused on renewal and customer attrition, we may decide not to include the parts of the life cycle relating to initial awareness of need/exploring options, as well as the initial negotiation and purchase process. The life-cycle stages we will map instead are: (1) ongoing use of the service; and (2) the renewal process. This will help us identify if we are losing customers at the point of renewal due to issues during ongoing use and/or during the renewal process itself.

For each stage of the life cycle that you are going to map, set up a section on your page, as in Figure 1.5, or a separate page.

During the Workshop

STEP 3: OVERVIEW AND INTRODUCTIONS

Start the workshop with a review of the problem statement and objective, making sure everyone understands and agrees. CJM workshops will involve multiple functions and/or departments, so this may be the first time many of your participants have met each other. Simply having all participants introduce themselves and briefly explain how their roles contribute to your customers' experience can help the team start to understand the journey of the customer.

Once aligned on the goals for the workshop, it's useful to also spend a few minutes talking about what you're going to map in this workshop, that is, the customer's journey, not your internal processes or tools that make up part of the ecosystem supporting that journey. Inevitably, participants will talk about their processes and internal pain points during the workshop. One way to manage and limit this is to draw a horizontal line about two-thirds of the way down your mapping page, whether that is on a whiteboard, flip chart, or digital medium. Explain that what is "above the line" is what is visible to the customer and what is "below the line" are the internal processes, tools, and systems that are not visible to the customer. Throughout the workshop, keep your notes separated into these "above the line" and "below the line" areas, with the focus primarily on the items that are visible to your customers.

F-Note: Prepare and follow an agenda but keep it high level to allow for flexibility in a dynamic workshop. For example, it could be as simple as:

I. Provide an overview and introductions

II. Inventory customer touchpoints

III. Identify moments of truth

IV. Evaluate pain points and opportunities

V. Develop an action plan

Above the line:

What is visible to the customer?

What are the customer's experiences, impressions, feelings, etc.?

Below the line:

What are the internal processes, tools, policies, etc. that result in the above-the-line customer experience even though the customer may not be aware of them?

Now it's time to actually create the CJM.

STEP 4: INVENTORY THE TOUCHPOINTS

Map the steps and touchpoints the customer takes during the applicable life-cycle stage. You can do this with sticky notes or digitally. If using sticky notes, put only one touchpoint on each square. A touchpoint may be an interaction with your company's personnel or with your product or services. This can be done through brainstorming, and you may also guide the team to generate touchpoint notes based on the customer stories you have gathered. You may even use methods from elsewhere in this book to facilitate compiling the list of touchpoints, as shown in Figure 1.6.

Organize the touchpoints chronologically to the extent there is a sequential order of touchpoints.

Figure 1.6 Sequence of customer touchpoints.

STEP 5: ANALYZE THE TOUCHPOINTS

Analyze each touchpoint using the following approach.

A. Identify whether the touchpoint is initiated by your company or by the customer. We like to use arrowheads to point this out.

F-Note: We like to use one color of notes for "mandatory" touchpoints, interactions that all customers have with us, and another color for "discretionary" touchpoints, which a customer may or may not have, in order to easily distinguish between these. Discretionary touchpoints may represent problem areas that cause undesired interactions.

B. Identify the purpose of the touchpoint from the customer's perspective (see Figures 1.7 and 1.8). Purposes may include to troubleshoot an issue, learn/receive training, transact business, confirm something, cancel a purchase or service, etc. It is useful to have a brief list of high-level purposes to select from consistently.

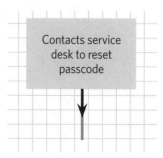

Figure 1.7 Showing touchpoint initiated by customer (arrow pointing from customer touchpoint box).

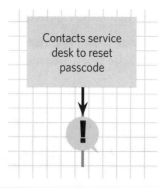

Figure 1.8 Showing touchpoint initiated by customer with an icon representing that the purpose is to troubleshoot an issue (using eVSM customer journey icon set—you can use any defined set of icons or labels).

C. Identify the method(s) of communication—telephone, web chat, email, face to face, survey, through an app or program, video, self-service, SMS text messaging, social media, web conference, etc.). The method of interaction may indicate a pain point of opportunity. For example, if the only way to contact your company's help desk is by calling, certain customers who prefer text messaging or other means of communication may be frustrated when trying to resolve issues.

D. Identify your internal program, function, service, personnel, or other contact point with whom the customer is interacting for this touchpoint.

E. Notate the customer's emotion or level of satisfaction during this touchpoint. Talking about the customer stories you gathered as prework may be helpful in this part of the conversation. Is this touchpoint an opportunity to turn a negative experience into a positive one for your customer? Are we frustrating customers at this point? How easy is it for them to get issues resolved? How often does an issue (touchpoint) occur? This is where personas start to be important—customer perceptions, feelings, and concerns may be different for each persona (see Figure 1.9).

F-Note: Certain touchpoints may be more critical to customers than others. Think about whether this touchpoint is one that MUST go right for a successful relationship with your customer. These are called "moments of truth," and it's a good idea to mark these with a star or other symbol.

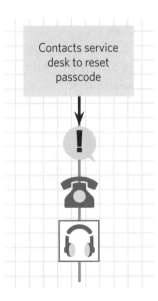

Figure 1.9 Showing touchpoint initiated by customer to troubleshoot an issue, achieved by calling customer service (using eVSM customer journey icon set—you can use any defined set of visual icons or text labels).

STEP 6: ADAPTATION—LABEL LEAN WASTES AND KAIZEN BURSTS

Now that you have inventoried and fully described your customer touchpoints, we find it useful to apply lean thinking and flag any touchpoints that are "waste" from a customer's perspective. Which touchpoints are the result of or involve any of the wastes? (see Table 1.6).

Defects (anything not done right the first time causes wasted time and wasted materials)	Transportation (pushing information to others or moving materials to another location)
Overproduction (making more than needed or more than the ordered quantity)	Inventory excess (too much in the IN basket so some items are not being addressed)
Waiting (approvals or prior steps take longer than expected or desired)	Motion waste (duplicate entry or searching multiple databases for information)
Not utilizing talent (confusion, knowledge waste)	Excess processing (gold-plating a silver order)

Table 1.6 The eight wastes of lean.

Any waste represents an opportunity for improvement.

As you discuss the touchpoints of the customer's journey, engaged workshop team members will state improvement ideas both to address identified pain points and also for expanded services and/or products. Flag these with a kaizen burst for identification in the next portion of the workshop.

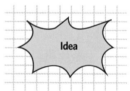

F-Note: The journey map can take on many forms. For automation or proactive management of the customer experience or other sophisticated objectives, you may want to consider journey mapping software. For simply documenting and analyzing the current state and opportunities, you can use a more standard software package or sticky notes on a wall. Process flowcharts can be adapted easily into CJMs as well.

STEP 7: ACTION PLANNING

As the facilitator, now is a good time to give participants a break in the workshop so you can review notes and pull together a list of the possible actions. List all the items that were tagged as either a waste or a kaizen burst from across the journey. Prioritize those that were also flagged as a moment of truth.

In the last part of the workshop, you will go through each of these possible improvement areas with the team and agree on an action to take. The actions will most often be changes "below the line" of visibility, such as updates to policies, processes, and tools. See the action register tool in Part 4 for an explanation of the possible types of actions: do it now, pilot test your solution, start a project, study further, or negotiate.

Be sure to close your workshop with a set of agreed-upon and prioritized improvement actions with owners, next steps/deliverables, and a timeline for implementation. Set clear expectations on how progress will be tracked through implementation. See Part 4 for a discussion on action registers. A completed CJM is shown at https://flexidian.com/customer-journey-map-examples/.

After the Workshop

Following the workshop:

- Send out documentation of the journey map, process maps, and action plan to all participants and key stakeholders.

- Schedule regular checkpoints to manage actions to completion.

- Measure the impacts through changes in the stories you hear from your customers as well as in quantitative metrics.

- Celebrate the workshop team's successes!

- Update the journey map periodically to reflect changes in the customer experience. As a best practice, it's good to update these annually (and when there is a major change in the process, the technology employed, or your organization).

The journey map documentation is also useful as training collateral. It can provide visibility on the full customer experience to employees across functions and helps promote customer centricity.

We were once in a meeting to prepare for a kaizen workshop with the managers of the four departments involved. The workshop was three weeks away and we were building the two-day outline. One of the managers told us there might be a bit of negativity in the room when we arrive. All the other managers jumped in quickly and expressed that the previous statement was far too polite and that we, as the facilitators, may run into a venomous mob, angry about the current situation in the workplace. We were not afraid.

WHAT'S IN MY FACILITATOR BAG?

I keep a small bag on hand for facilitating workshops. The key items I stock in the bag that may be handy in a workshop include:

- Sticky notes—lots of them and in a variety of colors and sizes
- Masking tape
- Scissors
- Colored-dot stickers
- Markers in a variety of colors and thicknesses
- Pens
- Whiteboard markers
- Whiteboard wipes
- Name-tag stickers
- Handful of USB memory sticks

See Part 4 for some tips on a virtual "facilitator's bag."

As a neutral facilitator, you have a great advantage: you can be perceived as an external observer with no hidden agenda and no motivation toward one set of changes or another. If you stay with our recommended approach of uttering *10 times more* questions than declarations, you will maintain that external, neutral, impartial perception from your audience.

Further, there are many ways to approach problem resolution, one of which is to nurture the negativity. Even with a group that does not visibly present a negative stance, we like to offer an opportunity to vent at the beginning of a kaizen workshop. Getting those arguments out in the open is your chance to hear firsthand the challenges and obstacles the group is facing.

F-Note: When negativity is expected, allow time at the beginning of the workshop for the team to vent frustration. Ask, "What are the obstacles we're facing right now?" Take notes and use these comments as input for later stages of the workshop. Cut off the venting after a specified amount of time. Tell the group, "Now it is time to look forward!" You are proving you are a neutral party.

Facilitator Kris's Journal—Mullins Heating & Cooling: Note 7

Days 5 and 6 at Mullins office: prepping for the customer journey workshop

As I prepared the team to map their customers' journey, we talked first about customer personas. The team decided to map three personas as focus areas:

1. *Home buyers purchasing an existing home with a previously installed unit within warranty and in need of repair*

2. *Homeowners in an existing home with an out-of-warranty unit needing repair or replacement*

3. *Homeowners with a recently installed unit (within one year of initial installation) who are experiencing issues*

We reviewed service records, complaint logs, social media comments, notes from our customer interviews, and focus groups – anything we could get our hands on to walk the gemba of the customer in preparation for the mapping workshop. Tomorrow we will apply the Kano model to our collected feedback to understand what drives customer dissatisfaction, satisfaction, and loyalty.

KANO ANALYSIS—USING CUSTOMER FEEDBACK TO IMPROVE SATISFACTION AND LOYALTY

The Kano model is a theory of product development and customer satisfaction that was created by Dr. Noriaki Kano in the 1980s. The model (Figure 1.10) uses two dimensions:

- Achievement (horizontal axis) with "not implemented" on the far left to "fully implemented" on the far right

- Satisfaction (vertical axis) goes from total dissatisfaction to total satisfaction

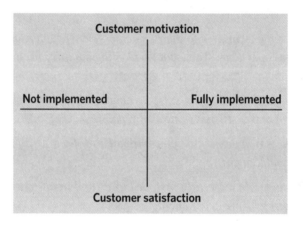

Figure 1.10 Example Kano model.

There are three levels of customer expectations represented in the model:

1. **Expected needs** (also known as "hygiene" needs) are the "must haves." Absence of these will create dissatisfaction. Presence will not increase satisfaction or loyalty.

2. **Normal needs** represent the customer's "wants." These are "satisfiers"—absence will cause customer dissatisfaction; delivering them very well can increase customer satisfaction.

3. **Attractive or exciting needs** offer the opportunity to innovate and delight your customers. While their absence is not a problem by itself, their presence can help strengthen customer loyalty.

Companies that deliver on the exciting needs on a regular basis are companies that develop very devoted followings.

At the core of the Kano model is also the reality that customer expectations increase over time. What delights customers today becomes expected tomorrow. The pace of increasing expectations is constantly faster, making it critical to identify and start developing toward tomorrow's exciting needs to deliver them before they are already part of the base expectations.

The Kano chart is a tool that has often been shared only briefly during a training class, mainly to show that customer delighters become must-haves over time. A more useful application of this two-axis chart is to plot the organization's current projects on the chart using the procedure and questioning guide described here:

1. List all the projects the team is currently executing and also those that are in the pipeline to be conducted next.

2. Draw the Kano chart using these labels:

   a. Write "customer motivation" at the top of the vertical axis and write "customer satisfaction" at the bottom.

   b. Write "low capability" at the left end of the horizontal axis and write "high capability" at the right end (see Figure 1.11).

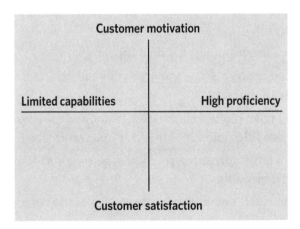

Figure 1.11 Setting up the Kano table.

3. Ask this set of questions for each project on the list, and plot each project on the Kano chart as you collect the answers:

F-Note: Give each project a number, and plot the projects using the project numbers on the Kano chart.

   a. Is this a short-term fix or a long-term innovation?

      i. If the answer is short-term, it belongs on the left side of the chart.

      ii. If the answer is long-term, it belongs on the right side.

   b. Are we basing this change on what our competitors are doing?

      i. If the answer is yes, the project belongs in the top left quadrant.

   c. If we don't make this change, will we lose customers?

      i. If the answer is yes, the project belongs in the lower half.

   d. Are we looking for a way to avoid future mistakes and failure costs?

      i. If the answer is yes, the project belongs on the bottom right.

      ii. However, if the approach is new and innovative, it belongs on the top right.

   e. Will we use Six Sigma DMAIC to solve this problem?

      i. If the answer is yes, the project usually belongs in the lower half.

   f. Will we use lean tools to solve this problem?

      i. If the answer is yes, the project usually belongs on the left side of the chart.

4. Once you have plotted all the project, look at the chart and assign these titles to each of the four quadrants (see Figure 1.12):

   a. Bottom left = correcting problems, getting into compliance, stop the bleeding

   b. Bottom right = avoiding future mistakes and costs of failure

   c. Top left = benchmarking, getting up to speed with the industry, standardizing processes

   d. Top right = visionary, innovative projects

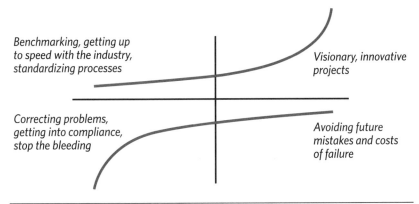

Benchmarking, getting up
to speed with the industry,
standardizing processes

Visionary, innovative
projects

Correcting problems,
getting into compliance,
stop the bleeding

Avoiding future
mistakes and costs
of failure

Figure 1.12 Kano chart project quadrants.

5. Your chart may look like this. Ask, "How does this profile of projects look to you?" Here are a few common observations and what they imply:

- An abundance of projects in the lower left requires the team to accelerate process improvement projects to improve capabilities and retain current customers. This is the space where the most basic customer requirements are not being consistently met.

- Benchmarking will often help the projects in the top left box. This box sometimes reflects a follower strategy or that an organization is trying to catch up to the market leader.

- Projects in the bottom right may require business process management and process control because capability is high at times, but the customer is only mildly impressed.

- Top right quadrant projects are good, though they still need to be managed for the innovations to be realized. There are often fewer projects in this box than the others (see Figure 1.13).

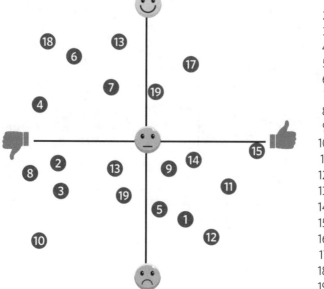

1. Finalize...
2. Implement...
3. Update...
4. Develop...
5. Finish...
6. Implement...
7. Benchmark...
8. Upgrade...
9. Update...
10. Eliminate...
11. Reduce...
12. Increase...
13. Develop...
14. Reduce...
15. Control...
16. Remove...
17. Test...
18. Discard...
19. Redeploy...

Figure 1.13 Example projects plotted on Kano chart.

Using this procedure, Kano analysis can help the team focus on what is important today and what is important for the future.

F-Note: Net promoter score (NPS) is based on a survey that asks customers their likelihood to recommend a service, product, or company on a scale of 0 to 10. Scores of 0 to 6 are considered detractors individuals who might spread negative word of mouth. Scores of 7 and 8 are passives, people who are neutral or might be satisfied but won't likely recommend to others. Scores of 9 and 10 represent promoters, or those who would likely recommend to others and influence additional purchases. The NPS score is calculated by first determining the percent of respondents in each category (percent promoters, percent passives, percent detractors) and then subtracting the detractor percentage from the promoter percentage. For example, if across 200 respondents, there were 100 promoters, 65 passives, and 35 detractors: 50% - 17.5% = 32.5 NPS score. Learn more at https://www.bain.com/insights/introducing-the-net-promoter-system-loyalty-insights/.

If you have a rated survey (NPS, customer satisfaction, customer effort, etc.), use the rating scale of the survey to help separate the customer verbatim feedback into the three types of needs in the Kano model.

For NPS, the categories are detractors, promoters, and passives. For other surveys that deploy a Likert-scale approach, separate the results into those who responded in the top box, bottom box, and the neutral midpoint respondents.

For each category of respondent, look at the verbatim feedback they offer in their survey comments (see, for example, Table 1.7).

	Expected needs	Performance needs	Delighters
If you are using the 10-point NPS scale	Lowest detractors, rating you 0–3	High detractors through passives, rating you 4–8	Promoters, rating you 9–10
If you are using a 5-point Likert scale	Bottom box, 1–2	Neutral midpoint is 3	Top box, 4–5

Table 1.7 Survey results mapped to Kano categories.

If you don't have a survey, consider other sources of feedback, including product reviews on shopping sites or social media comments. Look at feedback from competitor products and adjacent industries as well!

Facilitator Kris's Journal—Mullins Heating & Cooling: Note 8

Days 7–10 at Mullins office: workshop to action

Over the past several days, we scoured through customer survey results to determine what delights the Mullins customers (there were plenty of encouraging positive stories). The team decided to use these examples to establish a training program grounded in best practices and also to establish a rewards program for internals delivering excellent customer experiences.

We studied the more passive responses to determine some of the "make or break" points with customers, where doing a bit more might push the experience across the line into a promoter scenario.

We also looked closely at the worst of the feedback to get an honest view of where the team is losing customers.

Armed with the voice of the customer inputs from our survey Kano analysis, as well as from the customer interviews, we revisited the FMEA and refreshed our thinking on the issues list.

The Mullins team did a great job identifying issues and opportunities through the tools we deployed. Today was my last day in their office, and we wrapped up by creating an action plan to implement agreed-upon improvements to impact the prioritized issues in the FMEA. I will look forward to hearing their progress in our future checkpoints!

Kris's Progression

Whether you are starting a process improvement study or launching a new product or service, the tools presented here will help you gather customer requirements and prioritize actions. The sequence that has worked well for us and that we suggest for facilitators is as follows:

A. **Build the SIPOC.** You can start by drafting it yourself based on your knowledge of the work and your interviews with the operators. Then, with the team of people who play a part in this job, conduct a session to finalize the SIPOC. Leave nothing off the chart—it is better to study more variables and eliminate those that are not critical than to fail to include an element that may be important. Remember that the *output* column is not just a list of things that are produced; it must also include the measurable characteristics of each output, at least in terms of its *accuracy* and the *time* required to produce it.

B. **Play "my worst nightmare" (MWN).** To prevent negative occurrences, you must first understand what those negative conditions are. The MWN game enables you to find possible failures before they happen. Walk down each box in the center column of the SIPOC with your team and ask, "What problems can occur in this step?" This game is also useful for a group that tends to respond negatively to process improvement activities.

C. **Build the FMEA.** Now, the results from MWN can be studied further to define their level of risk in terms of their *severity*, their *frequency* or likelihood of occurrence, and their ease of *detection*. When these factors are multiplied, the product is the risk prioritization number, which is used to determine the sequence of problems to address. You may choose to build the FMEA yourself and then share it with the team for validation and refinement, because completing an FMEA form as a group may discourage maximum participation.

D. **Produce a customer journey map.** Walk the job from start to finish again, this time through your customer's eyes. You and your team will have a clearer picture of your customer's needs and even their feelings as they move through the full cycle from interest through purchase to use. Build it on a whiteboard wall or with mapping software, and enable the project team to view and contribute every step of the way.

E. **Add Kano analysis.** Use customer feedback to determine which customer needs are "must haves," which are opportunities to increase satisfaction, and which are ways to innovate and grow future business.

CLOSING THOUGHT—CRITICAL SUCCESS FACTORS

One of our assumptions is that you are a person who facilitates kaizen events or other types of workshops. You may have led hundreds already, or maybe you have only felt that exhilaration once or twice so far, or you may be somewhere in between. There are techniques that we have used and developed that have been helpful for us, and we will include many of these throughout this book for you to use, adapt, or file away as appropriate.

A very useful practice that we never fail to employ is the listing of critical success factors (CSFs) at the beginning of the workshop. You have probably heard that term — CSF — as it is common in Six Sigma training courses. It is usually defined as something like: *elements that are vital to the success of a strategy,* or *the variables necessary to ensure a positive result.* We've heard nicknames for them like "must-go-rights" and "the big rocks" (https://www.franklincovey.com/the-5-choices/choice-3.html). Our definition is: *the desired outcomes of this work for your customers, yourselves, and your regulatory authorities.*

To build that list, ask the kaizen event team, "What are the important and desirable outcomes of this work?" Tell the group to think of what is important to the customer, the company or organization, and to their regulatory agencies.

A list of CSFs for our facilitator's work with Mullins Heating & Cooling may be similar to Table 1.8.

Critical Success Factors		
Customer	Company	Regulatory
Timely installation	Get paid on time	Pass the annual audit
Reasonable price	Referral business	Pricing compliance
Updates throughout	Minimal punch list	
Clean house afterward		

Table 1.8 Critical success factors.

It is often easiest to start with the regulatory group because the reporting or auditing requirements your team may face are usually well understood. You can get the team talking by asking, "What regulatory requirements do you face with regard to this work?"

The customer list is usually next, because some of the people in the room will have heard, directly or indirectly, from customers who have expressed what is important to them, sometimes in very direct terms. The list need not be extremely long. It is a good practice to make the customer CSFs specific not vague.

For example, items like "communication" are usually too general to evaluate. When this topic arises, encourage the project team to be more specific by asking questions like:

- What kind of communication is needed?
- Where does communication break down?
- What frequency of project updates is preferred?

- What communication channels are preferred?

- How do you know if communication is sufficient?

The CSFs for the organization are sometimes a bit challenging to derive. First, which part of the organization are we talking about? Is it just the department that is doing the work or is it the larger body? Get the team to agree on that scope so they can list specific desired outcomes. The best way we have found to build this list is to ask the same question we described in the outputs discussion from the SIPOC tool described previously: How do we know that we've done a good job?

Write all the CSFs in a corner of the room or virtual workspace where they are visible but not prominent. By listing the CSFs and keeping them in view throughout the kaizen workshop, you are always able to point to them and ask, "Where in this workflow are we accomplishing CSF #1... CSF #2?" and so on. Later you can transcribe them to the project storyboard and show them near the beginning of a presentation.

If you have useful kaizen event facilitation techniques that you are willing to share with us, please write to us at info@flexidian.com. Thank you!

For a visual example of a customer journey map, see https://flexidian.com/customer-journey-map-examples/.

TRACY'S STORY

On a trip to Tokyo with a colleague who is from Nagoya, Japan, we decided to visit the Imperial Palace in Tokyo on Sunday. Not a frequent visitor to Tokyo, he was unsure where to park his car. He chose an empty parking lot near the palace, but a guard stopped the car from entering. The guard was immaculately dressed: pressed uniform, polished shoes, and white-gloved hands, one of which he showed us, fingers up and palm out, indicating that a stop was required.

In previous encounters of this type, I have experienced two common outcomes: one, the guard says something like, "We're closed," and that's the end of it; or two, the motorist asks for an exception with something like, "We're just going to be a few minutes." This experience was different: The guard approached my colleague and explained that the lot was being saved for a large group that would be arriving in a few hours, and then he instructed us where to park for the palace. He was extremely polite, and there was no way we were getting into the lot that he was protecting.

The customer interactions in your world must be the same—polite and firm.

- **Polite:** In all moments of truth, we have a chance to improve or damage the relationship. Be courteous and professional in all encounters.

- **Firm:** Customers need to know what to expect, and they deserve to know the reasons why the answer might be "No." If you make exceptions for some customers, the reasons an exception cannot be made for others may appear inconsistent.

For example, if your job is to collect applications from customers and evaluate them for approval, you must decide if you are going to accept incomplete or partial applications. If your policy is to accept only complete applications, but you take one that is incomplete as a friendly favor, your intentions may be very positive, but there is a problem: the applicant thinks you are working on it. They have already started counting the days until approval is awarded, but your staff may not have started to evaluate it because it is not yet complete.

Instead, if you politely send the customer back to complete the application before you accept it, and if you do this every time, then everyone will know the rule is being enforced, and they will bring only complete applications to your office.

There must never be a customer who is able to say, *"I got past the white gloves."* –T.O.

2

Innovate for Efficiency and Customer Experience

We borrowed this part's title from ASQ's Technical Community on Innovation, which was chartered in 2014 and has worked tirelessly to curate a body of knowledge on innovation management.

Many of the tools that are taught in a quality management training curriculum have become recognized and even standard around the world. To be sure, even the approaches to quality management have become much more consistent among organizations of all types and sizes over the last 25 years.

Innovation management is less standardized. While there are some themes and theories that have been promoted by companies that have generated many inventions, there continues to be inconsistency among approaches to innovation. Some restrict innovation projects to the research and development arm of the company, some only take on new project ideas from the C-suite, some still rely on a suggestion box, and still others have tried so many approaches that staff members pay very little attention to any program because it seems like the "flavor of the month."

What Is Innovation?

A useful definition of innovation is *the successful conversion of new knowledge into new products, services, and business models that bring value to customers.*

Picking this definition apart, we see that new products and services are a desired outcome of innovation. It also includes the importance of bringing value to customers, as well as the conversion of the idea into reality. Innovation is more than an idea or a spark. It needs to be delivered to bring value and to be appreciated as an innovation.

Innovations can also bring improvements that are realized internally, inside the organization only. It is important to focus on the end user, and the end user is not always an external customer. If the end user of your output is another department or agency within your organization, then the definition is still accurate!

The purpose of innovation management is to address an unmet need. This cycle begins with a creative impulse and concludes when that unmet need is conquered. It can begin again when a customer's needs change, when a new technology emerges, or when the next generation of the product or service is needed to stay ahead of the competition.

There are many ways to generate new ideas and many project management methods and tools that will help with execution and delivery. One tool for idea generation that we want to emphasize here is "flex hurdles,"[9] which is a great way to collect, evaluate, and prioritize ideas for action.

Facilitator Kris's Journal—Radisonville, PA: Note 1

Radisonville is a city of about 20,000 residents with one high school, 700 acres of green parks, two large company operations that employ about 3,000 people, and 60 miles of bike paths. The city government is concerned about development, wishing to keep the small-town feel but knowing that the high quality of life is attracting more and more people and companies to the area. Fear of overbuilding is juxtaposed with the desire to grow responsibly. One important factor in all this is for city officials to get the public's opinion on growth projects. The challenge: they can't seem to get residents, corporate representatives, and visitors to participate in open public meetings. At my scoping meeting with the city manager's staff, we discussed an approach to finding new ways to attract people to meetings, which I will facilitate with the larger city staff next week.

FLEX HURDLES—GENERATING AND PRIORITIZING GOOD IDEAS IN A SHORT AMOUNT OF TIME

The flex hurdles exercise is conducted with a group of people who want to make their product, service, or process better. They will

---

[9] Flex Hurdles is based in part on the second Innovation Game from Luke Hohmann: Speed Boat.

need to identify the factors that are holding back performance. To find those impediments, the facilitator draws a horizontal hurdle on the workspace and then describes the purpose of the game (see Figure 2.1).

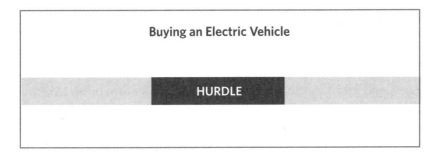

Figure 2.1 Initial setup of flex hurdles board.

The hurdle should be drawn across the center of the display space. This will leave room for the discussion points to follow. The facilitator explains that the hurdle represents the product or service that is being offered to customers, and that the product will not clear the hurdle because of trip hazards that will prevent it from leaping high enough. To get the hurdler running at top speed again, those trip hazards need to be addressed.

The trip hazards need to be identified and confronted. That is where this group's help is needed now. The facilitator asks the group to generate a list of possible trip hazards, for example, factors that may be causing the product to sell slowly or that generate negative feedback from customers. In short, the trip hazards are a list of the complaints participants have heard or think may occur about the product or service.

The game of flex hurdles begins with its focus on these trip hazards. Participants will be asked to write them individually on sticky notes and affix them to the display space directly. In a virtual setting using a conference whiteboard space, participants can type directly onto the display from their own desktops.

The facilitator next opens the discussion about the trip hazards and invites participants to explore the reasons for these trip hazards and the remedies or interventions that will remove or lessen their impact.

This discussion doesn't have to revolve around current products and services. In addition to trip hazards that are currently slowing the hurdle race, your team may need to evaluate future products to identify reasons they may fail to launch effectively.

In the game of flex hurdles, discussion of the trip hazards is followed by identification of the hurdle "boosters." Boosters are factors that can help the product or service be successful, boosting the speed and trajectory of the hurdler. The team will be asked to share these positive ideas as well.

Flex hurdles is an enjoyable activity that has been reliable in producing useful results, and it can be conducted using the description above. Our preferred deployment of flex hurdles takes this workshop a step further toward overcoming trip hazards and highlighting hurdle boosters more efficiently and effectively.

DEPLOYMENT: FLEX HURDLES

Scope Meeting

Before beginning to play flex hurdles, the objectives of the activity should be outlined. As the facilitator, you will be trusted to drive the team efficiently toward useful conclusions and an action register, which is a tool that will be described in detail in Part 4.

A scope meeting is important to set the stage for success during the activity. Meet with the manager of the department that performs the service you are trying to improve, or gather the cross-functional managers if more than one department is involved. Cover these items in the scope meeting:

1. The product, service, or process being examined

2. Elements of that product, service, or process that must be excluded from analysis, if any

3. Date, time, and location of the event

4. Participants (see the following)

The game of flex hurdles has been extremely useful in identifying many flaws and opportunities for improvement that may remain hidden without the participation of the group. But who should be included in this group? As discussed in Part 1 of this book, the SIPOC tool can help you decide who needs to be involved in process improvement exercises. The operators of the process, in other words everyone who plays a role in the steps listed in the P (process) column, should be represented. The C (customers) column—both internal and external—should be represented either in person, through recent VoC input that has been collected, or as personas the team has developed. The providers of inputs, who are listed in the S (sources) column, should also be represented during the flex hurdles activity.

F-Note: Hidden flaws can be a trap that causes improvement efforts to fail. As a facilitator, part of your job is to bring to light as many potential issues and downstream impacts as possible so the team can plan to remove or minimize the likelihood and severity of negative impacts.

The question now arises about whether the managers should be in the room. This will depend on the organizational culture and the interpersonal dynamics of the departments involved in the activity. The classic argument against having managers in the room is that people will be less inclined to speak freely about flaws and defects if the manager is listening. A strong argument in favor of including managers is that they will hear firsthand many complaints and issues that they may not have heard since moving into their managerial roles.

F-Note: Agree with the management team prior to the event that if the team seems reluctant to contribute any negative comments, you as the facilitator can specify a time during the exercise when the managers will exit the room, and the discussion will proceed without them. Anonymity is critical, so you must not identify the person who contributed any specific idea after the managers return for the debrief of the full flex hurdles exercise.

Flex Hurdles Workshop Preparation

Draw the hurdle on the display space and bring with you plenty of sticky notes in two colors: one color for trip hazards and one for boosters. Contrast in these two colors will be helpful, like yellow and pink, or orange and blue (see Figure 2.2). Write the name of the problem or opportunity at the top of the display so everyone can remember what is being discussed and not lose focus.

F-Note: Be aware of your audience when selecting contrasting colors to use. Workshop participants may have trouble distinguishing yellow from pink unless the yellow is a strong gold and the pink more of a hot pink. Orange and blue may be an easier contrast to detect.

Buying an Electric Vehicle

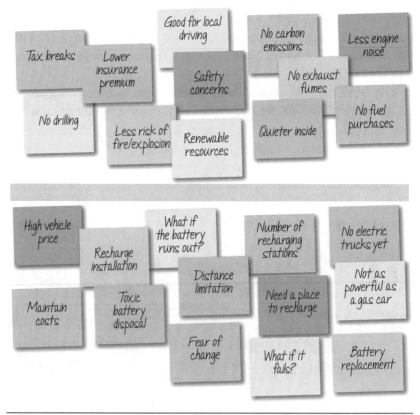

Figure 2.2 Flex hurdles for buying an electric vehicle.

Brief the participants that they are there to identify the reasons the product may fail or may not catch on, and that these are called trip hazards, as well as the factors that will cause it to be adopted and successful, called boosters.

Idea Generation

Begin with silent brainstorming. With only one idea per page of self-adhesive paper and using one color for trip hazards and the other color for boosters, instruct the participants that we need every trip hazard and booster they can provide to make the most of this project. Ask them to write these ideas down and bring them up to the display space. If you are in a virtual setting, ask that they be added to the virtual whiteboard using the chosen colors.

F-Note: Briefing participants in advance can help you save time during the workshop. You will still want each idea on a separate sticky note or as a unique entry. If they bring their ideas with them, that will reduce time spent thinking of trip hazards and boosters while in the workshop.

We suggest conducting this initial idea generation in silence to maintain focus and minimize the influence of more vocal workshop participants. It is also a good idea to remind the group that legible penmanship will be important for this exercise.

Offer a time limit for the idea-generation portion, but it's not always critical to stick to it exactly. It's more important to collect as many useful ideas as possible.

Once the popcorn kettle of ideas has stopped popping, you are ready to enter the next phase of the exercise. If, however, someone has another idea later in the workshop, encourage him or her to add it and not to keep it hidden. Those late-popped kernels can sometimes be the best!

F-Note: As with popping corn, ideas may come forward slowly at first. As the facilitator, you may need to do a little shaking to start the popping. If initially participants are slow to engage, ask probing questions, but remember to leave plenty of silence for free thought.

In a typical brainstorming exercise, the group would now begin to develop new ideas to overcome trip hazards of resistance. Each idea written would be read aloud by the facilitator, and the group would begin to discuss that item and decide what action to take. This is a useful exercise, but there are a few pitfalls:

1. It can be very time consuming to go through every single item. It is possible to lose your audience a bit when you are going over an item that may not concern everybody. The enthusiasm for discussing the first few items is almost certain to exceed the excitement of the group when discussing the last several items. This can lead to diminished thoroughness.

2. Many items will be repetitive. If two or more items truly say the exact same thing, there is no danger in putting them together and not discussing subsequent mentions after the first one. However, some notes will seem like they say the same thing and may be cast quickly into the "this is the same thing" net, when in reality there may be a difference worth discussing. For example, one note that reads *too many pages in the manual* and another that reads *too many materials to read* may seem at a glance like the same problem. But, there may be a different set of materials in addition to the manual, or the manual may not read clearly over a computer screen, or some other difference may exist that needs to be discussed. By lumping the two together after discussing the first, the chance to explore the second suggestion further is minimized. Additionally, the person who contributed that idea is still in the room and may resent the lack of discussion on that item.

3. The top priority item during the discussion may seem clear to everybody, but it can also be a side effect of that early enthusiasm. Or, the opposite may happen, and every new item will seem to be more important than the previous discussion.

These dynamics can be controlled. Our design for flex hurdles helps to guide the discussion toward a prioritized action list and will require two additional steps before discussion begins, as well as two more after the discussion has begun.

Flex Hurdles Analysis

Instead of moving directly into discussion after the trip hazards and boosters are placed on the board, let's spend a few minutes organizing and then prioritizing our thoughts and actions. Ask the participants to approach the display space and read all the notes posted silently to themselves. Then ask them to move the notes on the display into affinity groups. The affinity diagram, a truly foundational quality tool, is described in detail later, and that is what the group is creating on the flex hurdles board. Remind them that this part of the exercise—the reading and placement of sticky notes—is conducted in silence.

You will now have a flex hurdles board that looks similar to Figure 2.3.

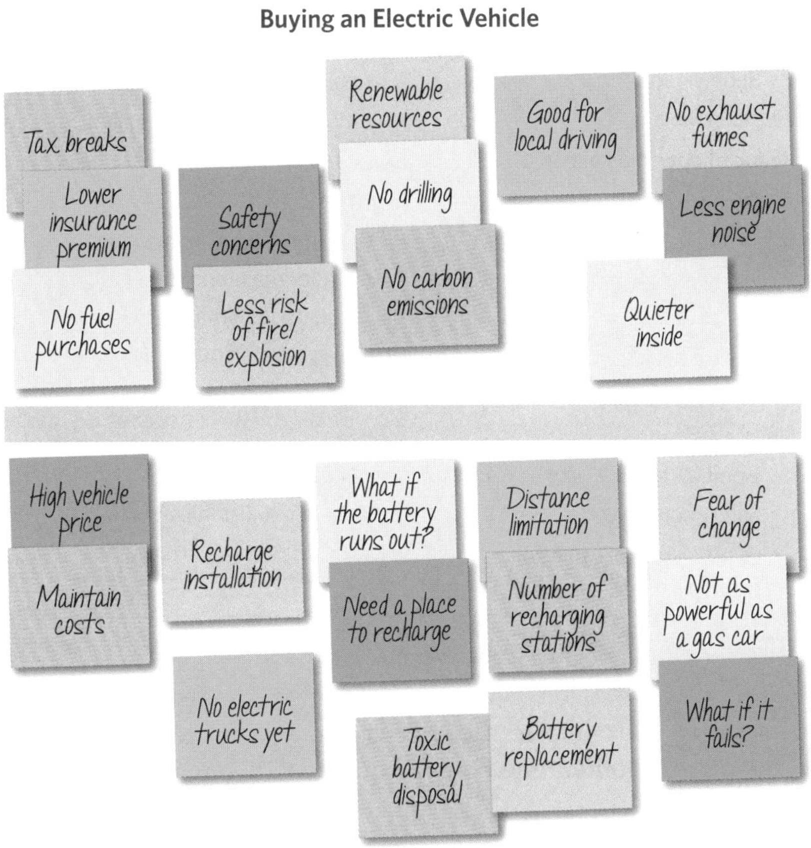

Buying an Electric Vehicle

Tax breaks

Renewable resources

Good for local driving

No exhaust fumes

Lower insurance premium

Safety concerns

No drilling

Less engine noise

No fuel purchases

Less risk of fire/ explosion

No carbon emissions

Quieter inside

High vehicle price

Recharge installation

What if the battery runs out?

Distance limitation

Fear of change

Maintain costs

Need a place to recharge

Number of recharging stations

Not as powerful as a gas car

No electric trucks yet

Toxic battery disposal

Battery replacement

What if it fails?

Figure 2.3 Flex hurdles organized into affinity groups.

F-Note: Participants should be empowered to move notes and rearrange each other's groupings during this silent exercise. The exercise is completed when movement stops.

As an example, the categories for buying an electric vehicle might include (see Table 2.1):

Boosters	Trip hazards
Environmentally friendly	Charge distance
• No carbon emission	• Distance limitation
• No exhaust fumes	• Need a place to recharge
• Renewable resources	• Number of recharging stations
• No drilling	• What if the battery runs out?
Reduced operating expense	Costs
• No fuel purchases	• High vehicle price
• Lower insurance premium	• Charge station installation
• Tax breaks	• Higher maintenance cost
Noise	• Expensive battery replacement
• Quieter inside	Uncategorized
• Less engine noise	• Toxic battery disposal
Uncategorized	• Fear of change
• Good for local driving	• No electric trucks yet
• Safety concerns	• What if it just fails?
• Less risk of fire/explosion	• Not as powerful as a gas car

Table 2.1 Example categories for buying an electric vehicle.

Now our flex hurdles activity continues. In part, our session incorporates another time-honored quality tool: force-field analysis.

REDISCOVER: FORCE-FIELD ANALYSIS

A vertical line is drawn in the center of a flip chart page or whiteboard to separate the space into two columns.

On the left are listed the driving forces: reasons a change will be supported by people it affects.

On the right are listed the restraining forces: elements in place today that will prevent the change from being accepted.

The team uses this discussion to identify driving forces that can be used to overcome specific restraining forces in order to adopt the change effectively.

DRIVING FORCES	RESTRAINING FORCES
Reasons the change will be welcomed	Reasons the change will be resisted
May include positive forecasts, morale-building elements, favorable customer experiences, and more	May include technical, political, and cultural factors that cause hesitation or reluctance

Force-field analysis is a tool used to find not only objections, sources of resistance, and obstacles but also positive factors that will influence the successful adoption of a process change or new program. It is commonly used by Six Sigma Green Belts and Black Belts during the improve phase of a project to help with change management and to drive acceptance of the new solution that the project team has developed and tested. The benefits of using force-field analysis are that the needs and opinions of stakeholders are brought forward for consideration, and also that the restraining forces are matched with driving forces that can be used to overcome them. Think of the force-field analysis as a list of boosters and trip hazards. This is where these two tools intersect.

In fact, our flex hurdles adaptation is the intersection of four tools: the flex hurdles workshop, the affinity diagram, the force-field analysis, and the clock diagram.

To create the final display on the flex hurdles board, ask the assembled team to take one more step. Instruct them to move entire affinity groups within the trip hazards to combine with affinity groups of boosters if any groups are related. We describe this part of the process as identifying both sides of the same coin, the positive and the negative.

For our electric car example, the team might combine the costs trip hazard group with the reduced operating expense booster group, because both are related to the financial aspects of the topic. While combining entire affinity groups, the team can also combine individual uncategorized ideas. For example, our electric car team may match the "good for local driving" booster with the charge distance trip hazard group because it is the same theme: driving distance. And they may add the "toxic battery disposal" trip hazard to the environmentally friendly booster group (see Table 2.2).

Boosters	Trip hazards
Environmentally friendly	• Toxic battery disposal
• No carbon emission	Costs
• No exhaust fumes	• High vehicle price
• Renewable resources	• Charge station installation
• No drilling	• Higher maintenance cost
Reduced operating expense	• Expensive battery replacement
• No fuel purchases	Charge distance
• Lower insurance premium	• Distance limitation
• Tax breaks	• Need a place to recharge
	• Number of recharging stations
• Good for local driving	• What if the battery runs out?

Table 2.2 Combined categories for buying an electric car.

The display space may look like this (see Figure 2.4):

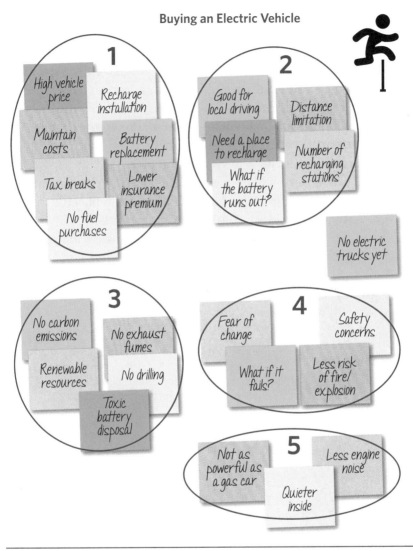

Figure 2.4 Final display space for flex hurdles on buying an electric car.

In the diagram, the name for cloud 1 might be cost concerns. Cloud 2 might be called driving distance. The names for clouds 3, 4, and 5 might be environmental concerns, safety and change, and comparisons to gasoline, respectively.

Action Planning

Why is it helpful to have the information organized in this way? You now have a matched set of factors: all these trip hazards need to be addressed, and right here on the chart you have corresponding boosters to help you make the argument and overcome resistance.

Through group discussion during this workshop, you may be able to add arguments that will help with adopting the change, and you may unearth even more possible causes of resistance. Add them to the chart and, ultimately, to your action plan.

Not all trip hazards will be overcome just by using the flex hurdles exercise to find the other side of the coin. Those trip hazards that are still not sufficiently addressed will need to be studied further. With this in mind, you may have five kinds of actions on the resulting action register (see Table 2.3).

Do it now	These are actions that are clearly defined and within our control. Implement them right away or on an established schedule.
Pilot test	These are actions we believe will help, but they need to be tested first to evaluate their effectiveness and ensure the solution causes no unintended or undesirable consequences anywhere in the organization.
Start a project	We know what the problem is, but we are not sure how to fix it. This is the time to start a process improvement project or an innovation campaign to determine the best intervention.
Study further	We don't really understand the full magnitude of the problem. If you are not able to articulate a problem statement describing the pain that is being felt today or detailing the gap between the desired performance and today's level of performance, then it is not time to start a project. It is time to learn the answers to those questions.
Negotiate	The solution we need is not entirely in our control. We must ask for help from other people or other departments, and we will have to present a convincing case for change.

Table 2.3 Five types of actions.

Before leaving the room, the team must agree to an action plan. See Part 4 of this book for more on action registers. Reserve time near the end of the workshop to agree with the team on the elements of an action register:

- What is the full list of actions that will be taken?
- Who is the accountable owner of each action?
- What is the next step for each of those actions?
- Who owns the next step?
- When will the next step be completed?
- Whose help is needed to complete the next step?

As the facilitator of this group, you must congratulate the team for developing such a useful set of output in a short amount of time. This is one of the main advantages of this adapted approach: the efficiency of the exercise. You may only need half a day to conduct this workshop and generate this valuable action plan (see Table 2.4).

Action	Action owner	Next step	Next step owner	Due date of next step	Support
Update priority messaging	Rui	Acquire list of current projects	Seza	February 12	Marketing
Build S&OP document	Marcella	Identify stakeholders	Marcella	February 26	Ops, Sales

Table 2.4 Short sample action register.

F-Note: Flex hurdles can also be played after the completion of a project, program, implementation, or product launch to discuss what went well and what obstacles were encountered. This can be helpful for a team to debrief and prevent problems in the future.

What's Next?

Correctly diagnosing the causes of a problem is an important step in solving that problem. Often the data analysis will lead you to a list of possible causes. Customer feedback will, of course, vocally point you toward problems that you can analyze, post-mortem style, to find out what happened. And the voice of the employee, your own staff, should play a significant role in learning what is really causing the problems you and your customers are facing.

There are many tools that can be used to identify possible causes. Before you take action, these identified factors need to be validated to prove they are, in fact, causing the specified problems you are trying to overcome. The diagram known as fishbone, Ishikawa, or cause-and-effect has been a reliable tool in this pursuit, and we've endorsed its usefulness for many years. The fishbone diagram was featured prominently in *Six Sigma Green Belt, Round 2*,[10] where Tracy called it a key ingredient for successful Six Sigma projects (see Figure 2.5).

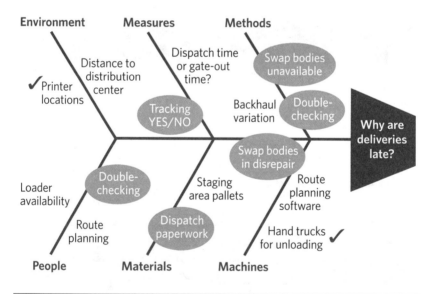

Figure 2.5 Fishbone diagram (borrowed from *Six Sigma Green Belt, Round 2*).

---

[10] Tracy L. Owens, *Six Sigma Green Belt, Round 2* (Milwaukee: Quality Press, 2011).

Building a fishbone diagram is usually easy once the names of the large bones have been determined. See https://asq.org/quality-resources/fishbone for more on fishbone diagrams.

You can use the six generic labels to get started—methods, measures, environment, materials, machines, and people—or you can select bone labels that make more sense for your project and then brainstorm with your team what specific elements are included in those categories. For example, a customer contact center that is discussing call abandon rate as a problem (using "Why is our mid-day abandon rate so high?" for the head of the fish) may choose to label the main bones of a fishbone diagram as breaks, call volume, support staff, system issues, advertising, and after call work, and then explore specific problems within each category. If you get the labels right, then the conversation flows smoothly. If you need to adjust the labels, remove one or more, or add new labels, a skilled facilitator can take that action easily during the discussion.

In practical application, for staff meetings or project team meetings, the decision regarding the labels of the major fish bones can be an obstacle to efficient deployment of the fishbone process. It may seem like a small matter, especially if everyone participating in the session is cooperative, but if anyone in the room is at all negative or opposed or reluctant, then one small hiccup such as the question, "What shall we name this fish bone?" can stand in the way of a productive session. Further, if someone has an idea that does not seem to fit into one of the bone categories, he or she may not share it with the group, and it may never get the attention it deserves.

F-Note: If using a fishbone diagram, as the facilitator you may want to label the major "bone" areas in advance of the workshop based on the subject matter at hand, so the team can focus on discussing causes and solutions in the workshop time.

Enter the affinity diagram. Using the affinity diagram tool, all the ideas of possible causes that are in the minds of the participants are shared regardless of what category they may or may not fit.

DEPLOYMENT: AFFINITY—CLOCK—SEQUENCE

Suppose a work team is trying to decide which problems to address first. Team members gather in person or in a virtual meeting and ask one another what issues should be fixed in their department. Each person is asked to contribute ideas.

If team members are meeting in person, they are given sticky notes on which to write down their ideas, one idea per square. Team members are instructed to put all their sticky-note ideas on a wall or flipchart. After everyone has posted individual ideas on the wall, there may be many sticky notes to sort through. This may look like a daunting, difficult job, and it may appear that department has lots of problems. A bit of skilled facilitation can make this exercise smooth and eye-opening for the participants.

Step 1: Silent Brainstorming

As mentioned previously, everyone will be asked to write on square sticky notes the elements of the overall problem being addressed.

Remind participants to write only one idea per sticky note. Multiple line items on one sticky note will not help you in the creation of the affinity diagram. Also remind the team that legible penmanship is important in this exercise!

F-Note: Write the problem statement on the whiteboard, or project it on a screen so no one loses sight of the issue you are tackling. The scope of the matter at hand can easily creep into other tangential or unrelated areas if you are not careful. This approach is equivalent to using the head of the fish in a fishbone diagram to keep everybody tuned to that specific problem.

As people finish writing, you can ask them to stick their ideas onto the wall, door, flip-chart page, butcher paper, large glass window, or the virtual whiteboard you may be using for an online work group. If anonymity is essential, then you as the facilitator can work your way around the room collecting all the notes and add them to the display space yourself. With a virtual group, you may have participants send their ideas to you so you can post them to the online display space. The added advantage to facilitator collection is that you will get to read all of them, or at least scan them, to get an idea of the content the participants are contributing.

Now all the contributed ideas are available for everybody to see, and seeing every one of them is important for step 2.

Step 2: Silent Arrangement

Here is our typical facilitator script to begin the next step: "OK, everyone please approach the wall and read each item that is written."

Be sure everyone is close enough to the display space that they can read all the comments.

Facilitator:

"Now, I want you to move all the sticky notes and arrange them in groups of items that are related. You need to actually pluck them from the wall and move them together. For a group to be considered a 'group,' they must be touching."

F-Note: One thing we never do in this kind of session is to point at a specific comment and ask, "Who wrote this?" Part of the value in this exercise is that anonymity is preserved through the use of silent written comments.

Asking for the individual notes to be put into groups brings about construction of the affinity diagram, so you must make that part clear before beginning and then remind them during the exercise.

Facilitator:

"Oh, one more thing… this exercise is done in silence."

This practice of silent collaboration has always worked for us, because it helps to prevent any dominant or vocal team member from exerting too much verbal influence on the group. Even in groups without such a dominant voice, it is still possible to fall into groupthink when someone shares a comment like, "Oh, those four are really the same, let's put them together."

F-Note: If creating the affinity diagram with a virtual project team, do some research ahead of time to select an online tool that meets your needs and is compatible with your conferencing technology.

Indeed, groupthink is possible even without vocal participation. Some items can be grouped with others because they seem similar, but a group of heterogeneous items does not help achieve the purpose of the exercise, which is to pinpoint specific opportunities for improvement. So, the next line in our script is:

Facilitator:

"Before you finish, please take a look at any group that has five or more items in it and see if it can be subdivided."

This is helpful for breaking down ideas into specific topics. For example, the team that was outlining arguments for and against the use of electric vehicles began to put all items related to costs into one group on the affinity diagram that resulted from their game of flex hurdles. Initial costs, however, are different than ongoing costs, so items like vehicle price, recharging station installation, insurance costs, and vehicle maintenance expenses should be classified separately and targeted separately for improvement or, in the case of that flex hurdles team, for messaging.

Step 3: Grouping and Naming Clouds

Now the affinity groups are clear and separated. At this point, we usually tell the group that they can at last speak, and they are usually quite relieved.

Before the team leaves the display space, there is one more step required to complete the affinity diagram. Each affinity group now needs a name. Ask one of the participants to draw a circle or cloud around each group. Then ask the full group to give a name to each of the affinity groups. A sample affinity diagram is shown in Figure 2.6.

F-Note: The size of the group will help you decide how best to construct the affinity diagram. If the working team is small, that is, less than 10 people, then it should be no problem to follow the instructions as one group. If the number of participants is larger than 10, some modifications will be needed. As they approach the display space, some players will gravitate to the front, and others will stay in the back. After one minute of silent arranging, say to the group, "OK, it has been one minute. If you are in the back, please move to the front, and if you are in the front, please roll to the back for the next minute." This is helpful so everyone has a chance for their unspoken voice to be heard on the affinity diagram. An advantage to creating the affinity diagram with a remote virtual team is that they do not encounter this physical space limitation.

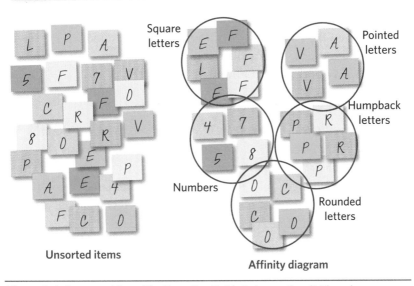

Figure 2.6 Borrowed from *The Executive Guide to Innovation* (Milwaukee: Quality Press, 2013).

F-Note: Individual ideas that don't fit into any circled category should be analyzed separately. Avoid creating a "miscellaneous" group if possible; ask the team to decide whether those ideas should be analyzed further or set aside as out of scope.

Naming the groups can follow any format that the group likes, but if process improvement is your goal, give each group a name that is constructed as VERB—OBJECT. For example, in an exercise trying to identify process improvements in the office of a chiropractor, the affinity group comprising Table 2.5 could be named "upgrade waiting room."

Uncomfortable chairs	Slow WiFi	Queueing at check-in
Entrance door hits desk	Old magazines	

Table 2.5 Chiropractor's office improvement opportunities.

The visual diagram on the display space that includes groups of related ideas that are circled and named is the affinity diagram. This tool alone can be useful in determining necessary actions for a team. However, the question of prioritization usually arises at this point: "OK, this is a good list, but where do we start?"

Facilitator Kris's Journal—Radisonville, PA: Note 2

Last week I facilitated a game of flex hurdles with the Radisonville city staff. Out of the exercise, we ended up with a healthy list of ideas on overcoming trip hazards and maximizing boosters that will help the city grow while maintaining their beloved small-town environment. They entered the items into an action register. This morning I got a call from the team again—one of the key members of the small city staff team is out with an illness, and it's impacting their ability to deliver all the agreed actions. They would like to work through a reprioritization of the actions. When I go back on-site with the team this week, I'll introduce the "clock diagram" as a device to support them on this. We already have the affinity groups from flex hurdles, so we'll jump right into clock diagram completion.

Step 4: Clock Diagram Completion

Initiatives or projects can be prioritized in many ways: Impact and effort, multivoting with dot stickers, a Hoshin X-Matrix, weighted criteria scoring, and more (see Table 2.6).

Impact/effort matrix	High effort required	Low effort required
High impact expected	Projects in this box will bring high impact but will need a high level of effort. These should be the No. 2 priority.	This is the No. 1 priority area for projects. Ideas here are high in impact and low in effort.
Low impact expected	Low impact and high effort is the last type of project you want to pursue, unless the project is needed for regulatory, safety, or other urgent reasons.	Low impact and low effort are typically "pet" projects. Some wins are available here, so don't discourage them, but they must not interfere with the box above.

Table 2.6 Impact and effort matrix.

F-Note: Feelings can be hurt when someone's favorite project is put in one of the low impact boxes. Be sure to follow up with those individuals to discuss options. You may be able to offer support for completion of such projects separately and then publicize those success stories.

One method of prioritization that we have found useful is the pairwise comparison of individual projects using an interrelationship digraph, commonly known as the clock diagram. Picking up from the affinity diagram just created, the clock diagram is easy to set up, and the discussion that takes place while completing it is usually rich with details that help the team prioritize projects thoroughly.

The name of each cloud or theme from the affinity diagram (for example, upgrade waiting room) is transferred to another space—a whiteboard or new flip-chart page, or perhaps a new document if the meeting is being conducted virtually. The theme titles are arranged in a circular shape. See Figure 2.7 for an example of what the themes from a doctor's office affinity diagram might be.

Any number of themes or initiatives can be evaluated using the clock diagram. We call it "going true clock" when there are 12 items being discussed.

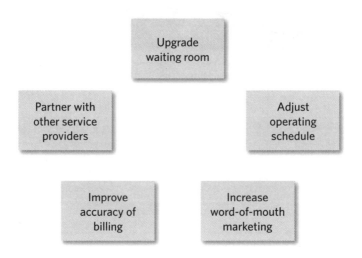

Figure 2.7 Clock diagram initial setup, doctor's office.

Next, the team assesses the relationship of each pair of items, beginning at the top of the clock and proceeding in a clockwise direction. In the previous example, the first pair evaluated is "upgrade waiting room" and "adjust operating schedule." The team will debate which of those two needs to be addressed first.

Because it is more important for a new driver to learn to operate the vehicle than it is to learn to refuel the vehicle, the arrow between these two items points to operate vehicle.

Rules of the road wins the head-to-head matchup with the other two because one must pass the written test before taking the driving test.

F-Note: Sometimes a sample clock diagram is useful in demonstrating how the tool works. Figure 2.8 is one we have used to introduce the clock diagram.

To evaluate the items in pairs, the facilitator asks the question, "Which of these items needs to be addressed first?" The correct answer to that question may not be known to the facilitator prior to this discussion, nor does it need to be. The facilitator's job is to ensure it is discussed thoroughly, understood by all, and agreed via consensus before moving on to the next pair.

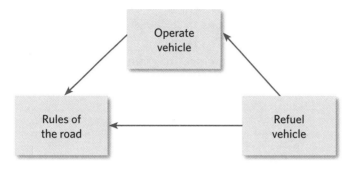

Figure 2.8 Simple example of a clock diagram for teaching a new driver.

For each pair, an arrow is drawn with the arrowhead pointing to the item that must be addressed first. That decision may be based on a few factors, and the facilitator must ask the best question to help the team decide. Here are the questions we use:

- Which of these two needs to be fixed before the other can be fixed? (Remember we are only evaluating two items against each other at any time.)

- The successful execution of which of these two items leads to the success of the other?

- Which of these two will be easier to fix or more beneficial? (Think of the impact and effort matrix above.)

The last step in building a clock diagram is to count the arrowheads attached to each item and write that number next to the theme title. Figure 2.9 shows the doctor's completed clock diagram. You can see that "improve accuracy of billing" brought four arrowheads and "partner with other service providers" lost all its pairwise evaluations.

One additional note on facilitating the clock diagram discussion: Sometimes is may seem difficult to explain the use of the arrow no matter how many times you repeat the three previous questions. It can be useful to go through the first set of pairwise comparisons and then pause to ask the group, "Have I explained the clock diagram well enough?" and go back through those first several evaluations to validate the consensus by saying, "You agreed that [item X] needs to be addressed before [item Y] because the arrowhead is pointing at [item X]. Is that correct?" If revisions are needed, make them now before completing the full clock diagram and then realizing that it was not fully understood throughout the process.

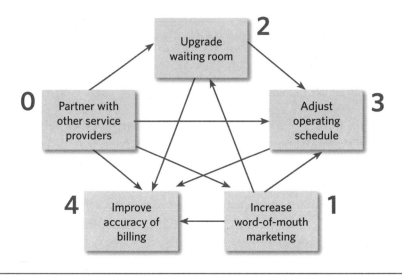

Figure 2.9 Completed clock diagram, doctor's office.

Step 5: Extracting the Sequence

Starting with the largest number of arrowheads and ending with the lowest number, list the theme titles in order.

In the aforementioned example, "improve accuracy of billing" will be listed first because it has four arrowheads touching it in the clock diagram. The descending sequence of numbers is now the team's prioritized list of projects or processes to improve.

F-Note: Do not discard the original notes that the team generated during the first step, silent brainstorming. Those individual items will be shared with the eventual project team to use in studying the situation and pursuing the best solution.

Prioritized list:

I. Improve accuracy of billing

II. Adjust operating schedule

III. Upgrade waiting room

IV. Increase word-of-mouth marketing

V. Partner with other service providers

Is it possible that one of the lower items may jump to the top of the list after the clock diagram is built? Yes, there may be an urgent need that arises later, or there may be an organizational priority that was not revealed during this process that requires higher prioritization. Or, as indicated in the impact vs. effort matrix in Figure 2.6, there may be a regulatory requirement or a safety-related item that must take a higher priority. You, as the facilitator, must handle these changes with aplomb and describe them openly and honestly to the group.

What do we do in the event of a tie? If two items have the same number of arrowheads touching them, precedence goes to the item with the arrowhead when it is matched with the other item having the same number. In Figure 2.10, items B and D in the diagram both have a score of 3, and the arrow between B and D points to B. Also, the arrow between A and E points to A, so the final sequence is B−D−C−A−E.

This progression of tools from affinity diagram to clock diagram and sequence is versatile, too; it is useful not only in the identification of problems that need to be addressed but also in an innovation or new product introduction setting. Picture the cross-functional team identifying critical elements of a new service for customers and struggling with which items to address first. With some useful inclusion of the VoC, the team will be able to prioritize their initiatives in an effort to bring the service to market and get it right the first time.

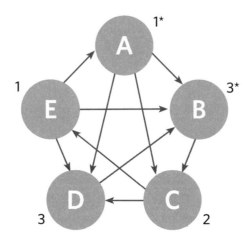

Figure 2.10 Completed clock diagram.

Facilitator Kris's Journal—Radisonville Sales Team

Inviting new companies of any size to locate their offices and operations in Radisonville is the mission of the city of Radisonville economic development staff. The contracts the city can sign with new organizations may include such benefits as access to training for employees, corporate wellness programs, a period of reduced taxes, and more. Some of these options are easy to approve, and there are some other requests that the sales staff makes that are not possible to offer. The city manager's office finds itself denying common requests over and over, and they are also burdened with some requests that the sales team should be able to address without their assistance. I will propose the response router tool for their use.

RESPONSE ROUTER—DON'T WASTE TIME
APPROVING AND DENYING THE SAME THINGS

Why do they ask us the same questions over and over?

This is a problem that we have encountered in many settings.

Often it is expressed by a company's legal staff when sales contracts are being negotiated, and the sales agent sends all the customer's questions to legal for review and approval, including many questions that are decisions that need to be made by the business leaders, not the legal team.

At other times, these repeated requests are actually against the rules, and the sales agents should have been briefed by the sales leaders who should know by now! At least that's what the attorneys have told us.

Legal departments are not the only targets of unnecessary questions. The quality department may be asked if a batch of parts can be shipped even though it does not conform to specifications (NO!). The safety team could be asked for permission to enter a part of the factory that is clearly not under any sort of restriction (GO!). The senior leaders may be asked to support a new initiative, but the project team has not proven that their pilot test was successful (SHOW us the data!). And a drill sergeant might be asked by a young private for permission to speak when the answer every time is, "Yes! Speak! And make it fast, we have a lot to do!"

How much time do you spend responding to questions that:

- Have already been answered the same way many times?

- Have a published answer in the manual or on the website?

- Arrive *after* the relevant decision or action was needed?

This is a waste of time and energy, and it is a source of frustration. But there is a way to avoid this problem, and it just takes a little bit of time to prepare and share: the response router tool.

Picture a list of issues: a list of issues that a team member can read and that outlines which questions they do not need to bring

F-Note: In this, as in several other settings, the tool can be prepared as a draft in advance and then shared with the project team for validation. If you are able to converse with the decision makers and ascertain their responses ahead of time, then a large portion of the work will already be done!

forward. Specifically, the "green" list of questions where the answer is already known to be "yes" are questions that should not be asked repeatedly. Wouldn't that be a time saver? As long as people don't abuse the list and take liberties, it should save a lot of time. For this reason, the "always yes" list needs to be very clear about what specific approval is being granted.

At the same time, what about a list of items that team members should not even bring up because the answer is always "no"? Even though they might not like that answer, publishing such a list is still a time saver.

The inevitable question regarding the "always no" list is, "Why not?" The "always no" list should have the answer to that question listed; it is only fair. You can even go further and offer a proposed alternative that the agent can take back to the requestor to advance the discussion after the initial request is disapproved. If the "always no" list is prepared conscientiously and shared proactively, your team member who is managing this requestor or customer will be armed with approvals, disapprovals with reasons and alternatives, and will know the boundaries in this negotiation.

Not every question will fit neatly into an "always yes" or "always no" list. This is the province of the third part of the response router: the negotiate category. There are two types of requests that are listed under negotiate:

- Specific items that require further discussion, fine tuning, or escalation before they can be resolved.

- Anything new that is not already on the response router should go into negotiate until a blanket yes or no can be determined, and then that item is moved into the appropriate list.

Table 2.7 shows the response router completed for requests made to Radisonville's economic development department. A success story for the use of the response router tool:

A local hardware store was experiencing revenue loss from an increasing number of returns. Upon review, it was discovered that several of the weekday salesclerks, seeking to please customers as well as being conflict adverse, were accepting returns without receipts and without question. In fact, they had even given cash back on returns purchased at a different store. Many of the accepted returns could not be reshelved due to their condition and other factors. We worked with the manager of the store to create a clear response router chart and posted it visibly at the checkout counter. This freed the clerks from having to make decisions about returns and empowered them to easily say "yes" or "no." The "always yes" category included unused items in original packaging accompanied by a store receipt. The "always no" category included damaged items and items with visible wear and tear. The "negotiate" category was replaced with "at manager discretion" and included items such as new items in original packaging not accompanied by a receipt (for example, items received as a gift). After implementing the response router tool, the store saw a 70% decrease in returned items, reversing the flow of revenue loss that was previously due to returns.

Always yes	Negotiate	Always no	Reason	Alternatives
Requests for on-site corporate wellness program for one year	Reduced corporate taxes for XX months	Indemnification	The city's insurance prohibits this clause.	Suggest an arbitration clause using Radisonville city code/laws.
Access to city's fitness facility for all company employees for the first three months	Employee training by city staff; opening position is "not offered"; escalate to city's organizational development staff if needed	Deviations from code for new construction	The city's strategic plan includes vision for new construction and is strictly enforced.	Remind applicant that approval is fast-tracked if all documentary requirements are met upon initial application.
Donations by company of less than $500 for city events		Free fitness facility use for all employees for more than three months	The city's insurance prohibits fee-free use of athletic facilities beyond 90 days.	Negotiate a reduced rate for months 3-12, the maximum discount is 50%.

Table 2.7 Sample response router for Radisonville, PA, economic development.

Facilitator Kris's Journal—Radisonville Building Permits: Note 1

Once an agreement is struck for a new company, there is often the need to build a new structure for their use. Several teams must work together to review, advise, and approve the developer's request, and this process often takes longer than the developers would like. Neighboring cities, as a benchmark, can complete architectural review and zoning approval faster than Radisonville, and this has led to the loss of several contracts over the years. To get everybody on the same track, I will conduct a milestone mapping workshop with the various departments including zoning, planning, engineering, inspection, and traffic. It might also be a good idea to invite one or two builders or developers for part of the workshop to get their input directly. I'll ask the city staff how they feel about that.

MILESTONE MAPPING—SUCCINCTLY TELL THE SAME STORY TO EVERYBODY INVOLVED

We have discussed in this book a few different ways to map a process. This new method is simple, easy to build and understand, comprehensive yet succinct, and quietly making quality management more accessible in many work environments.

Milestone mapping is a tool that we have commonly used during the improve phase of a Six Sigma project or during the process redesign portion of a kaizen event. Once the current process has been mapped with a SIPOC or flowchart, and the red flags that impede progress have been identified through value analysis, waste analysis, and fishbone charting, the new way of working must be designed and agreed.

F-Note: 5W2H is sometimes referred to as "the reporter's questions." It includes:
Who?
What?
When?
Where?
Why?
How?
How much or how often?

Rather than drawing a full, new swimlane diagram to depict the new process, the milestone map may be more expeditious and easier to follow, especially when everyone in the workshop or on the project team has already been discussing and analyzing the current state and has helped to build the list of obstacles. Building a new, complete process map may seem like an unnecessary burden.

F-Note: The milestone mapping technique is useful when a project team has energy around a future state design but may suffer from process mapping fatigue after building the detailed process map at the beginning of the kaizen workshop.

The milestone map (see, for example, Figure 2.11) is a collection of the major deliverables of the work process that is being studied and redesigned. At its core, it is a 5W2H analysis of each of these milestones, and to construct it requires just a few simple facilitation steps:

1. Remember we are mapping the new workflow. The milestone map is not commonly used for mapping a current state process because it doesn't usually reveal enough details to be helpful in evaluating work for waste, non-value adding steps, and red flags.

Milestone 1— Application 5W2H	Milestone 2— Site Plan 5W2H	Milestone 3— Plans Reviewed 5W2H
Who? Developer/builder	**Who?** Developer/builder	**Who?** Building department
What? *Complete* application	**What?** Finished plat submitted	**What?** Review to building code
When? Need 30 days prior to economic development deadline	**When?** Within 15 days after application is received	**When?** Decision and documents needed within 21 days
Where: Must send to city hall	**Where:** Send to zoning	**Where:** Leave at desk for pickup
How: Electronic filing is recommended	**How:** Electronic filing is required	**How:** Paper signature required
Whom to notify? Building department must be informed on EC-2	**Whom to notify?** Building department must be informed on EC-2	**Whom to notify?** Inform economic development on EC-2 spreadsheet

Figure 2.11 Sample milestone map sheets for Radisonville building department.

2. Agree with the team on the list of major steps and deliverables from start to finish of the work that is being improved. One good place to find a starter list of milestones is under the P column in a well-constructed SIPOC.

3. Attach one piece of flip-chart paper to the wall for each milestone and label it at the top. Write "5W2H" near the top, to remind everyone that you will be asking those questions for each milestone.

4. For each agreed milestone, ask the project team this series of questions:

   a. Who is responsible for completing or executing this milestone?

   b. What exactly is the deliverable?

   c. When is the time frame that this deliverable is needed?

   d. Where will the work be done or sent?

   e. How does this deliverable need to be built, filed, executed, etc.?

   f. *Finally, we always add:* Who needs to be informed when this deliverable is complete?

5. The most important thing in milestone mapping is that everyone agrees to follow these new rules. Just like developing a new flowchart in the improve phase of a Six Sigma project, the milestone map is a commitment to a new way of working. Don't let anyone leave the meeting until that agreement is made.

6. You, the facilitator, must promptly document the results of this discussion and share the milestone map with all parties who need to know.

Facilitator Kris's Journal—Radisonville Building Permits: Note 2

We completed the milestone mapping workshop for the Radisonville building permits department, and the process is now running smoother than ever. I went back to the city office 90 days after implementing as a follow-up, and the team reported that not only are they experiencing an increase in successful contracts, but other city departments have also implemented simple milestone maps. In fact, this approach has become a standard best practice for all project work in the city! With this and other improvements we've implemented, neighboring cities have begun to take note, and Radisonville is becoming the new benchmark.

To reprise: Innovation is *the successful conversion of new knowledge into new products, services, and business models that bring value to customers.*

While the tools and approaches to innovation are less standardized than those of the quality management discipline, by adopting a set of flexible tools, you can facilitate innovation in a structured way that increases the rate of conversion from ideation to value for your customers.

3

Execute and Measure

THE SOUND OF CLOSING DRAWERS

When you have identified your customers' needs, quality management continues by constructing the best flow of work to deliver those needs fully and timely.

Part 1 of this book was built to highlight the importance of fully understanding the needs of your customer and beginning to translate them into your workplace so you can meet those needs every time. Part 2 was about generating new ideas for delivering value to those customers. Part 3 now switches the focus to the internal efficiency of your team in producing and delivering your customer's order. The leading tools that are employed to make sure your team is expending as few resources as possible to meet customer needs is the methodology known as lean thinking.[11]

In lean thinking, only the work that is necessary to meet customer needs is considered to be of value to your customer.

For our purposes, we'll define "value-adding process steps" in this way: *Any step in the process that either produces the value or delivers the value to the customer.* Any other step illustrated on the process map is considered non-value adding and is a target for elimination or minimization.

Non-value-adding work can create busyness with the illusion of productivity. As we have told many of our workshop participants over the years, "Not using lean techniques is like chopping wood with a shovel:

You'll build up a good sweat, and you'll see a lot of chips flying, but there's really a better way."

---

[11] Available lean references also cover lean manufacturing, lean office, lean production, lean enterprise, lean kaizen, lean startup, lean product, lean impact, lean turnaround, Lean Six Sigma, and more.

5 PRINCIPLES OF LEAN

Sharing with your audience that lean is a constructed methodology and not just common sense can be very useful when beginning an improvement project. Womack and Jones* introduced the five principles of lean in the 1990s, and they are still relevant today. Inform your working group about these ideals:

1. Define VALUE in the eyes of the customer. In plain language, the reason your customer called you—whatever it is they have asked of you—that is the value, the thing that needs to be delivered.

2. Map the VALUE STREAM. The set of materials and information required to deliver the value is the value stream. Simply put, it is the combined set of resources that are required to produce and deliver what the customer needs.

3. Optimize the FLOW. Now that you've listed everything you need to acquire and execute to produce the value, arrange all of that in the best sequence to deliver the value while expending as little resources (energy, time, money, raw materials, inventory) as possible.

4. Let the customer PULL the value. Don't work ahead, don't make more than you have to make, don't provide a service that was not requested, and don't wait until you have a batch of work to begin doing it. The concept of pull means you work only when work is required. We like the sound of that!

5. Pursue PERFECTION. After you've taken the four measures above, go back and do it all again, because customer needs can change, new technology evolves, and process reengineering is a positive approach for any organization.

*The Machine that Changed the World (New York: Simon & Schuster, 1990)

Facilitator Kris's Journal—Elm Grove Volunteer Lawyers Program: Note 1

I received a note from my friend who is a practicing attorney at a downtown law firm. She volunteers about six hours each month to this community program (shorthand: EGVLP) that helps people—primarily low-income families in the local area—with their legal issues. She says it's very rewarding work, and she's happy to do it, but the EGVLP has not *always made the work easy because they are a bit disorganized. She and the other volunteer lawyers have two main complaints:*

- *They can't find the materials they need quickly in the EGVLP office.*
- *The EGVLP is not able to provide reliable tracking of volunteer hours for reporting.*

My playbook for this project:

1. Evaluate the office layout.

2. Establish 5S for organization.

3. Develop an initial set of performance metrics.

FLEX 5S—NOT JUST FOR FACTORIES AND TOOL ROOMS

A useful tool in the pursuit of efficient workplace operation is 5S. The traditional approach to 5S was built for use in factories and tool rooms. It does not always resonate in a workplace filled with cubicles and databases. The tool itself can still prove useful in that type of setting, but the approach needs to be modified. The flex method of 5S deployment is applicable in nonmanufacturing environments and will help you save time and be more productive.

The Basics

The topic of 5S is taught to students of lean as five Japanese words that begin with the "s" sound and that have been translated into English words that also begin with the letter S. The first three words: seiri, seiton, and seiso are really the practical tools that drive productivity and time savings. The fourth and fifth words—seiketsu and shitsuke—are more about practicing the first three all the time and turning 5S into a significant part of the organizational culture.

The 5S approach has proven invaluable in factory and tool-room settings, saving time, energy, cost, and space, and even promoting a positive impact on employee safety. If you don't work in a factory, however, the traditional translations of 5S may not provide much value for you.

5S: THE TRADITIONAL TRANSLATIONS

First S: Seiri, 整理, defined as "collating" or "sorting," usually translated to "sort," meaning that you decide what is important to your work and keep those items close to you. Conversely, identify the items you don't need as often and move them away from you to save time and space.

Second S: Seiton, 整頓, defined as "tidy, orderly," usually translated to "set in order" or "straighten." Once you've sorted your materials and tools, put them in a place where they can be found when needed, and replace them there every time you use them.

Third S: Seiso, 清掃, defined as "cleaning," usually translated as "sweep," "shine," or "scrub." In a tool-room scenario this means you clean your tools after using them so they will be ready for use the next time you reach for them.

Fourth S: Seiketsu, 清潔, defined as "cleanliness" or "the state of being clean," usually translated as "standardize." The first three S words need to be practiced all day, every day, and seiketsu promotes 5S becoming a habit.

Fifth S: Shitsuke, 躾, defined as "discipline" or "upbringing," usually translated as "sustain." Now that you've begun practicing 5S, make this a program and not a one-time act by using incentives, audits, and employee input to emphasize the positive results of deploying 5S.

The Flex Approach

To really underscore the value a 5S culture can bring to a non-production environment, an approach that blends the traditional basics with a more service-oriented view is needed. As the facilitator or leader of a team applying 5S, flex the 5S just a bit to increase the value:

1. Flex your overview description of 5S, depending on whether you are working with the team on overall workplace organization, such as on a manufacturing floor, or in an individual contributor environment where there is more personal control over one's work space and methods (see Table 3.1).

2. Start with the first "S," sort. Flex your approach depending on whether you are dealing with a production or service environment (see Table 3.2).

F-Note: Don't be alarmed if someone in your team meeting says something like, "Oh, sure... 5S... that means you put a label on your desk where your stapler goes!" while rolling the eyes sarcastically. When 5S is introduced to a group, it is normally taught with the factory mindset, part of which includes marking locations for tools and cleaning the area on a regular basis. The flex 5S approach is revised and adapted for offices. Assure your group that this is not just a tool for tool rooms!

Traditional approach— Present an overview	Flex approach— Present an overview
5S are five Japanese words that begin with the "s" sound. They've been translated into English verbs that also begin with "s," and they represent a step-by-step approach to workplace organization.	5S are five Japanese words that begin with the "s" sound. They've been translated into English words that also begin with "s" and that describe an approach to individual workspace discipline that will save time and effort every day.

Table 3.1 Initial introduction to flex 5S.

Traditional approach— Sort	Flex approach— Sorted
The tools that you will definitely need when you get to work are worn on your tool belt so they are handy, within reach. Other tools that you might need are left in the toolbox because you don't want unnecessary items in your way. This is "sort," keeping only the necessary items near you and moving other items out of your immediate area.	"Sort" is all about determining which of your documents, tools, supplies, and references are necessary frequently vs. only for occasional use. Sort by importance as well as frequency of use. Determine which of your files, both physical and digital, are needed on a regular basis and which are saved for longer-term needs only (for example, audits, potential discovery, etc.). Take the same approach with your email. Which email do you need readily on hand, and which messages are you saving for future reference only?

Table 3.2 Sort changes to sorted.

3. The second "S," set in order, is also easily flexed, as shown in Table 3.3.

4. For the third "S," shine, our flex approach adapts a different translation. This is the most significant difference between the flex adaptation and the traditional 5S approach. While the Japanese word seiso connotes cleanliness, the use of cleaning products and brooms does not resonate as a process improvement method in an office environment. Table 3.4 presents the distinction between the cleaning aspect of seiso and the need to ensure your tools and materials are all serviceable. Our point is, no matter what you are working on, you must use only the most current, most accurate, and "cleanest" version of that product.

5. The fourth "S," standardize, means that the first three "s" words need to be applied all day, every day, as described in Table 3.5.

6. The fifth "S," sustain, is about making the 5S a regular program rather than just a periodic "spring cleaning" or one-time effort. 5S becomes part of our organizational DNA (see Table 3.6).

Traditional approach— Set in order	Flex approach— Set in place
Once you have decided which items to keep close to you, always keep them in that location so you can find them quickly every time they are needed. The items that you've decided to move to another location must also be put back into that spot where they can be found easily every time you look for them.	Once you have decided which items to keep close to you, always keep them in that location so you can find them quickly every time they are needed. Set your files in the place you need them for ready access. Create physical and/or digital files for your documents. In a digital environment, keep shortcuts or bookmarks to those you use daily on your desktop in an organized location while storing those needed only occasionally in a file structure that does not clutter your desktop. When you open and edit documents, store them back where they belong. Don't create multiple versions in different locations. In a physical file environment, consider putting files that aren't needed regularly into a storage area that is not in your regular workspace. Keep critical daily files close at hand. For email, keep only email demanding near-term action in your inbox. File all other notes into intuitive folder locations for future reference. As new email comes in, sort each note and set it in an appropriate location.

Table 3.3 Set in place for flex 5S.

Traditional approach—Shine, sweep, scrub	Flex approach—Serviceable
Your tools must be ready for use every time you reach for them. Clean as you go, and finish any job by cleaning your tools.	Your files and resources need to be ready for use at all times. Have you ever had a magazine subscription and let the whole stack of issues build up in a messy pile? Don't let outdated resource manuals overtake your office. Keep only the most current and up-to-date version of any documentation.
	Implement a version control approach, especially for shared files. Make sure all stakeholders have ready access to the same "source of truth" and are not confused by outdated copies of files.
	If multiple people need to access information about a customer, service incident, case, etc., make sure all relevant notes and pertinent information are stored together in an organized location—sticky notes on one person's desk aren't accessible broadly.
	Digital notes using a shared approach work better and keep the file more serviceable.

Table 3.4 A big difference between seiso in traditional 5S and in flex 5S.

Traditional approach— Standardize	Flex approach— Standardized
5S should not be a special project or effort; it should be part of a daily habit. Every person and team, whether they work in a truck, at a desk, in the tool room, or on the shop floor, must practice 5S every day to maintain the high level of organization that will keep the operation running smoothly.	The first three "s" words are really the habits that need to be formed to save time and stay organized. Seiketsu is your effort to make the first three Ss a recurring set of actions. Apply your version control and file storage/update practices in your daily work, making organization a habit.

Table 3.5 Standardize the approach to flex 5S.

Traditional approach— Sustain	Flex approach— Sustained
Make this a part of the way you do business by rewarding 5S behaviors. You will know that you have a good 5S program when you never have to tidy up the work space for a high-ranking executive or a customer visit.	The Japanese word shitsuke is usually presented as "sustain" in English, but it actually translates to "upbringing" or "child-rearing," which takes the depth of this fifth "S" to a new, more profound level. It is part of the very fiber of our organization and must be reinforced to prove that it is. Make it a part of your employee onboarding, ongoing training, and incentive programs to bring up employees with 5S ingrained in the corporate culture.

Table 3.6 Sustain the behaviors to build the culture.

Sometimes a sixth "S," safety, is added. In a manufacturing environment, there are often physical dangers, and workplace safety is a priority. Safety principles are also likely to apply in an office environment, as well as other nonproduction facilities. However, we do not presume to educate on safety topics while our focus is promoting process improvement (see Figure 3.1).

We are often asked, "How can we improve the culture in our organization?" Responding in this context and remembering that 5S is foundational to an organization's ability to make lasting, positive changes, we respond that a culture of 5S does not grow overnight. The first three S words are good habits that need to be practiced regularly, so they become routine behaviors. Once those behaviors have set in, or become standardized, then the culture begins to form. Sustainment of these positive behaviors leads to a culture of quality.[12]

Figure 3.1 Habits are the foundation for behaviors, and behaviors form the basis for culture.

---

[12] Thank you, Marshall Sherman!

The Benefits

Why bother with 5S anyway? Well, picture this: you need to revise a document and, as soon as you reach for it, it is there. Then you need to research a specific customer's history with your firm, and the database you need to study is open, current, and ready for your eyes. Next you have to

F-Note: In a quality workshop, when establishing a new work process or refining an existing process, ask the team what inputs and outputs of the process require sorting, setting in place, and maintaining serviceability. The improvement plan should include these aspects.

update a monthly report, and the sources are all accurate and up to date, plus this month's draft report has already been prepared for you to add the new information. How much time would you save each week? And what would you do with that time?

We ask this of all the groups we meet: If together we could find 10% of your time that could be released and given back to you, how would you spend it? One good answer to that question is to spend more time in the top right box of the Kano analysis we covered in Part 1 of this book!

How do we achieve these lofty goals? Specifically, for a team workshop, here are a few initial streams of questioning that you can use to introduce 5S.

1. First ask, "How much time do you spend looking for files?" They will groan or chuckle and say something like, "It's hard to count that high." A primary lesson of 5S and lean thinking is that if you spend a little extra time at the beginning, you will save a lot of time later. You will also reduce headaches, frustration, cost, and customer dissatisfaction. In this case, the way a file is named should be a primary target. Take a minute to give the file a useful name in a recognizable format. For example, one group we assisted agreed during the workshop that all sales quotes would be labeled with the two-digit year, the first four letters of the sales agent's last name, a hyphen, the first four letters of the prospect's name, and the Julian date the quote was prepared, like this: 19GIBS-RADI221 (for a quote by Laura Gibson for Radisonville on August 9, 2019).

2. Similarly, images are often difficult to find, and one frequent reason for this is the name of the file: IMG000019, IMG000021, or IMG000022. Ask, "How much time do you waste looking for image files?" It can take a long time to go through a list of images with that kind of file name, opening each one to see if it is the one you want. Take five seconds when saving the photo or image and give it a name you'll recognize later, like TracyInCave.jpg.

3. Next, inquire of the group, "How many times do you have to reproduce a report for someone?" When you build a report and send it via email to another person or a list of people, you are pushing that report, and it takes time for you to do that. When that report is updated, then you have to send it to all those people again. Plus, if someone else wants the report, you must take time to send it again. Instead, post that report in a central location where all who require it have been granted the necessary access. In addition to simplifying your job and saving time, you can also ensure that only the most current version of that report is being consulted and used, because you will update it in its saved location when necessary.

4. "How difficult is it to find files in your file structure?" Most of us use shared file folders, and those folders can get filled with files that are no longer current. When you update a file, remove the previous version from that location so it is not an obstacle to performance. Depending on your document retention rules, you will either destroy the previous version or archive it in a separate location for a period of time. Either way, you will move it away from the folder where you and others will be looking for the most current version.

5. "How much time is lost searching databases?" Team members whose job it is to answer questions often have to search for the answers to those questions. If they have to search in multiple locations or databases, that consumes time and delays the completion of the task. Take the time to organize the locations that are required for research into one resource, one database, or one virtual repository of all the information they are likely to need.

6. Finally, challenge the group with, "Is your office supply closet organized like your home junk drawer?" For those offices where actual tangible items are moving from one place to another, like in a supply room, organize everything so people who are looking for something can find it at a glance, and so there are fewer locations to consult when searching for the needed item. Not only will everyone save time, but you will also save cost because you will have less need to overstock, and people will not hoard office supplies. Admittedly, the sound of opening and closing drawers in the supply room can be pleasant for some, but it is usually an indication that 5S is needed.

Facilitator Kris's Journal—Elm Grove Volunteer Lawyers Program: Note 2

I visited the EGVLP office and shadowed the staff for the day, keeping notes on the office layout, including both physical and digital organization.

I observed the following opportunities:

- *All client files are kept in the same storage area on the main floor, including both active and past cases. They take up an extensive amount of space within the primary work area, making the office feel small and cramped.*

  - *Recommendation: Sort the files into active and past cases. Keep only the active cases in the main area. Sort inactive files by year. Store only those that are required to be stored (documentation retention policies), and shred those no longer needed. Move the inactive case file storage to an alternative storage area (closet) that is not on the main floor. Consider digitizing records where possible for improved storage capabilities.*

- *When volunteers and staff access a file, they often then leave it on their desk or other workspace rather than returning it into the file cabinet.*

  - *Recommendation: Set in place—implement a practice of returning files to their sorted and designated location as soon as possible after use. A few minutes spent returning the file to the location reduces clutter as well as ensures the file is updated and accessible for others who may need it. Too much time is wasted today searching for files* on someone's desk when they are unexpectedly out of the office. Setting the file back into place will also reduce confusion when documents are erroneously placed into the wrong file folder due to multiple folders sitting at someone's desk.

- Most of the staff and volunteers jot down notes about active cases on sticky notes or in notepads. Appointment times and other details are on slips of paper on desks or stuck to the sides of computer monitors. This has resulted in appointments being missed as well as other errors and duplicated effort.

  - Recommendation: Serviceable—cases are more readily serviceable when all associated notes are kept up to date in a common location. Consider digitizing all notes in one place per case following a standard approach. This will reduce loss of notes, increase legibility, and improve audit trails. If notes cannot be digitized, at least file them promptly into the correct case file folder.

- Office supplies are spread throughout the office. Staff members spend a lot of time throughout the day looking for staplers, sticky note pads, pens, etc. One individual was observed giving up the hunt and placing an order to purchase new notepads only to find a stack of unused supplies in a cabinet in the conference room later that day. While the EGVLP budget is tight, a significant portion of it goes toward repeat purchases of office supplies.

  - Recommendation: Sort and set in place—gather together office supplies into one storage cabinet. Organize the cabinet, creating a space for each type of supply. Implement a process of ordering new supplies only when inventory runs down to a designated level. Implement a practice of only removing supplies from the cabinet as needed and returning unused supplies to their designated location. Once the storage and use of supplies becomes more habitually organized, supply costs will decrease.

I also created a brief training module on 5S habits the EGVLP can use going forward to educate staff, especially new team members, interns, and volunteers, so 5S becomes both habitual and ingrained in their daily operations.

During the COVID-19 pandemic of 2019–2020, many business offices around the world had to suddenly adjust to a sustained work-from-home environment. For those relying on sticky notes, printed files, and unorganized offices, this was a monumentally challenging shift. Creating organized digital file structures, work notes, and a well-maintained 5S office space supports greater work location flexibility.

5S — A Closing Thought

As a closing thought, here is a point of view that we have shared in workshops when the topic of inefficiency has arisen and 5S is discussed as a remedy:

If any of your work is inefficient or you have customer complaints, and the workplace is also disorganized, adding structure and discipline to your operations is a necessary first step before real process improvement can take hold.

Not knowing where materials are kept, not having access to necessary information or databases, not using the most current version of a file, and not being able to find anything in your teammate's area when that person is out of the office—these are time wasters, these explanations for failure are too easy, and they are easily prevented with the use of 5S. 5S is like brushing your teeth: you do it every day, and it is the foundation for good oral hygiene.

Facilitator Kris's Journal—EGVLP—Note 3

After working with the team on implementing 5S, I next took a look at their reports in order to work toward producing a set of performance metrics.

To evaluate the effectiveness of the EGVLP, there are two major reports that they produce every month:

1. Case completion report: This is a two-part document including:

    a. Executive summary with informational tables and charts showing the number and types of cases completed in the previous month, the total number of volunteer hours recorded, the expenses incurred by the program, and the sources of funding

b. *Case details that show conditions (with all names redacted) and outcomes of each case with comments to help EGVLP prepare for later cases of the same or similar type*

2. *Volunteer hours report: This is a table listing the volunteer lawyers, the number of cases they've handled, the number of hours they recorded in support of each case, and a comments field describing the outcome of each case*

These reports take several hours to compile each month.

FLEX OEE—MORE COMPLETE THAN A SIMPLE PRODUCTIVITY MEASURE

"What are your performance metrics?" is a question we ask when we are getting to know a new client.

The answers are myriad:

- Sales per agent
- Calls per hour
- Average order size (dollars per sale)
- Return on investment (ROI, that is, dollars earned per dollar spent)
- Average handle time (total time spent on the phone divided by the number of calls; time per call)
- Acquisition cost (marketing and onboarding spend per new customer)

We've chosen to list a few examples of ratio-type metrics, each one having a "per" included.

As a matter of fact, any productivity metric is a quotient:

Productivity is the amount of output generated for an amount of input consumed or used. It's simple and elegant, and it's very useful when tracking the progress your work unit is making.

$$P = \frac{O}{I}$$

Are we getting better, are we getting worse, or are we standing still?

These questions are answered when comparing the ratio metrics over time.

In Figure 3.2:

This graph

looks better
than this one

and this one
is best, right?

Figure 3.2 Comparing productivity using line charts.

Remember that we are referring to productivity measures, meaning the amount of useful work that is getting done using the inputs provided. "Up" is always better in productivity, and there are two ways to make the "P" in our equation increase:

1. Increase the output at a higher rate than the input is increasing.

   a. Output increases as input stays the same.

   b. Output increases by a factor of x, and input increases by a factor less than x.

   c. Output increases and input actually decreases.

2. Decrease the input at a faster rate than output is decreasing.

   a. Input decreases as output stays the same.

   b. Input decreases by a factor of y, and output decreases by a factor of less than y. Said another way, if output is decreasing by y, then input must decrease by a rate faster than y. Productivity improvement is possible even during a period of decline.

   c. Input decreases as output actually increases.

Tracking performance using data and graphs like these is fine for showing past performance and current trends, but it has been said that managing your organization with these tools is like driving a car while looking only at the rear-view mirror. The next dot on your graph may surprise you if you are only looking at the past.

To promote process improvements while tracking productivity, we need to look for targeted improvement opportunities. A chart like those shown previously does not give us enough clues to study for improvement.[13] To enable managers, supervisors, and team members to identify not just *when* productivity declined but also *why* it did, we introduce a variation on another time-honored manufacturing method, the measure of overall equipment effectiveness (OEE).

MEASURE OF OVERALL EQUIPMENT EFFECTIVENESS (OEE)

OEE is a metric that is used to track and compare the productivity of a specific manufacturing machine over time. More importantly, it is used to describe in detail the causes of productivity gaps.

There are three components to OEE, and each is expressed as a %.

- **Availability.** Given the amount of time the machine could have been running, how much time was the machine running? The calculation is:

  Actual time/Max available time

- **Performance** (or efficiency). Given the amount of time the machine was running, how many pieces did it produce compared to how many pieces it could have produced? This requires a knowledge of the ideal time needed to produce one piece. The calculation is:

  [Ideal processing time x
  Number of pieces produced]/Actual time

- **Quality.** Given the number of pieces produced during that time period, what proportion of them were made correctly the first time without any need for rework? The calculation is:

  Good parts/Total pieces

When multiplied together, these factors determine OEE.

A x P x Q = OEE

(continued)

---

[13] One erroneous clue that is too often derived from a time series chart is when a dot dips below the average or does not increase from the previous dot. We have seen too many occasions where a manager will see a dot drift and react: "What happened?!" This is typically a waste of time because a sustained period of upwardly mobile dots should not be an expected phenomenon. For more on this topic, see: Donald C. Wheeler, *Understanding Variation: The Key to Managing Chaos* (Knoxville, TN: SPC Press, 2000).

MEASURE OF OVERALL EQUIPMENT EFFECTIVENESS (OEE)

Example:

85% Availability x 91% Performance x 78% Quality = 60% OEE

By the calculations, you can see that 100% is the theoretical maximum.

Accepted levels of OEE are:
100% = Perfect
85% to 100% = World class
60% to 85% = Common, with room for improvement
40% to 60% = Low productivity

Each of the components—availability, performance, and quality—reveals causes of lost productivity, known as the six big losses:

Within the availability component, there can be losses in two areas:

Breakdowns—The machine stops running due to maintenance failures.

Changeover—The switch from one part to another takes longer than planned.

In the performance component, losses are found in:

Reduced speed—The job is taking longer than expected.

Minor stops—They are not to the degree of a breakdown or changeover.

For quality, losses are found in:

Startup defects—Sometimes the first few pieces are not up to standard.

Scrapped pieces—Those that fail inspection or are obviously defective.

When used outside of manufacturing, the mention of OEE immediately turns off our audience because we are not machines. So, normally we don't even say "equipment." To keep the OEE label, it would be easy to translate to "overall employee effectiveness," and we have used that naming many times. Sometimes, however, the team associates a negative connotation to the word "employee." If that is the case in your world, you are free to change the name to "overall staff effectiveness," or whatever label works best for you.

OEE FOR THE OFFICE—FLEX ADAPTATION OF OEE

We start with the same basic measurements: availability, performance, and quality.

The key is in the operating definitions of each of these terms.

For availability, instead of measuring machine run time, define the measurement as:

Actual work time/Maximum available time

F-Note: When facilitating a process improvement workshop, you should address not only what changes are to be implemented but also how effectiveness will be measured. OEE is a useful device in this. Discussing and implementing OEE avoids the pitfall of deploying processes that are overly complex for employees to follow and maintain efficiently.

So, if someone is potentially able to work eight hours in a day, but due to outside appointments, unscheduled meetings, or other considerations only actually works six hours in that day, his or her availability is simply 6/8 or 75%. This measurement can be taken over any desired time period and either at an individual or group level. For example, if across a team of five full-time employees within a 40-hour work week, two people each spend three days on a special assignment and all other time is worked, the availability of the team was (3 people x 40 hours + 2 people x 24 hours)/(5 people x 40 hours) = 168/200 = 84%.

F-Note: Ask the group, "How do you measure productivity?" The answer will likely be:
a) The count of items completed
b) The number of items completed over a specified period of time (items per hour, for example)
c) A group measure of total items completed divided by the number of team members (items per operator)
OEE controls for the time period by eliminated nonworking time from the items per time metric.

If desired, you may want to make the measurement more granular, for instance, accounting for breaks or other nonproductive time. If employees arriving at work take 15 minutes at the start of their day getting a cup of coffee, talking to coworkers, and otherwise settling in to start the day, that is 15 minutes that could be counted as part of the maximum available time and not the actual work time. We would just caution that when you go down this path, maintain your awareness that humans are not machines! A human being attempting to be actually working at all times during a workday with no breaks would soon experience burn out and frustration.

While 100% availability is still the theoretical maximum, the target for the team and/or individual should be set considering allowance for breaks, meetings, training classes, and other time away from work.

For efficiency, a few elements need to be defined:

- Number of pieces produced—Think about the various types of work products a team or individual produces. These could be pieces of code from a computer program developer, reports produced, customer interactions completed in a contact center, patients seen in an urgent-care office, etc. Instead of using the standard terms "pieces produced," flex your operating definition to meet your business.

> F-Note: It is critical to get alignment on the definition of each element with the project and operating teams. Don't assume an agreed definition exists. State definitions explicitly to avoid otherwise hidden differences in interpretation.

- Ideal processing time—With human processes in service environments, there is often much more variation in "processing time" than when a machine is producing widgets. For instance, a restaurant server taking customer orders is likely to find that some customers place their orders quickly and efficiently, while others take more time studying the menu and asking questions. Conduct an analysis of your average processing times for the same or similar work. Consider whether there are seasonal or time-of-day differences. What other factors may impact processing time? Set your ideal time based on your historical data to allow for expected variation. Note that the basis for ideal process time may be different for members of the same team if some are handling simpler work and some are working on more complex items, as described in the Table 1/Table 2 tool section later.

- Actual time—Use the same actual work time as in the equation above for availability.

A few examples of efficiency when measuring human processes:

- A nurse practitioner saw eight patients in a day. Through record keeping, we see that a patient visit is ideally about 30 minutes. The nurse practitioner worked six hours that day. His efficiency was (30 minutes x 8 patients)/6 hours. Standardizing all the time elements to minutes for easier calculation, this becomes (30 x 8)/360 = 240/360 = 67%.

- A contact center employee handled 70 customer calls in a day. The ideal handling time for a call of the type this employee handles has been established as five minutes per call. The employee worked seven hours in the day. Her efficiency was (5 minutes x 70 calls)/7 hours = (5 x 70)/420 = 350/420 = 83%.

- A lawyer met with five clients in the day. Each client meeting is budgeted one hour. The same lawyer that day had two court appearances at 30 minutes each. She drafted three briefs, with the ideal standard at her firm being 45 minutes to produce a brief. The lawyer worked a long 10-hour day. Her efficiency was ((60 minutes x 5 clients) + (30 minutes x 2 court appearances) + (45 minutes x 3 briefs))/10 hours = (300 + 60 + 135)/600 = 495/600 = 82.5%.

For quality, you will need to define what in your business is equivalent to a "good part." What constitutes "right first time" vs. something needing rework? For example, in a contact center example, a customer who needs to make a second contact to get an issue resolved would be a contact requiring rework. Consider the output of the process (see Part 1 SIPOC discussion on output). What defined a "good" output? The calculation of quality for our purposes here should be all good output divided by the total quantity of all output (good and bad).

F-Note: Not every item produced or completed is always done correctly the first time. OEE includes the quality of work, because defects lead to rework and scrap, which is a strain on the system.

Always ask the team, "What happens when the work is not done correctly the first time?"

A few examples of measuring quality in this context:

- A restaurant server took orders for 40 customers during his shift. Three diners sent back their food because they received the wrong items, and two diners demanded items be excluded from their bill because the food was cold and not to the expected standard. Of the 40 orders, 35 were "good" (no issues), resulting in a quality measurement of 35/40, or 87.5%.

- A technician installed four air-conditioning units in a day. The next day, one of the customers called to complain the unit was not working. The technician had to go back to the site to make repairs. Her quality rating on installation of these four units was 75%.

- A plumber made six customer service visits. All six were resolved satisfactorily, with no complaints. The plumber's quality rating was 100%.

As with traditional OEE, the overall effectiveness in the service scenarios is measured by multiplying Availability x Efficiency x Quality.

The six big losses also can be flexed to fit the nonproduction environment as well (see Table 3.7). In all cases, keep in mind that a low OEE requires root cause investigation to isolate, mitigate, and improve the process. It should not be assumed that poor OEE is the "fault" of the employee operating within the process. For example, a restaurant server with a poor quality score due to orders sent back to the kitchen may be experiencing the impact of a poor chef or bad ingredients rather than a fault within his or her control. The OEE calculation gives an indication of the area of potential improvement.

Availability losses	Time fully out of work	Downtime within work time
Traditional definition	Breakdown—The machine stops running due to maintenance failures.	Changeover—The switch from one piece to another takes longer than planned.
Flex definition	Time off—Last-minute assignments, sick, and other time completely away from the office (planned or unplanned).	Unscheduled breaks, setup time at the start of the day, time switching from one job task to another.
Performance/ efficiency losses	Reduced speed	Minor stops
Traditional definition	The job is taking longer than expected.	Delay in work, not to the degree of a breakdown or changeover.
Flex definition	The job is taking longer than expected.	Delay in work, for example, waiting for a response from someone else, or other pauses not as significant as downtime/break.
Quality losses	Startup defects	Scrapped pieces
Traditional definition	Sometimes the first few pieces are not up to standard.	Pieces that fail inspection or are obviously defective.
Flex definition	Defects resulting from new process implementation, someone being new to a process, lack of training, or similar "getting started" issues.	Work product requiring rework, resulting in customer complaints or escalations, repeat inquiries to resolve an issue, or any output that is rejected by the customer.

Table 3.7 OEE traditional and flex definitions.

Facilitator Kris's Journal—EGVLP: Note 4

Applying the concept of OEE at Elm Grove Volunteer Lawyers Project, we reworked their two volunteer hours report into a volunteer OEE report that we named overall program effectiveness (OPE). The new OPE report provides stronger, more actionable insights than the old volunteer lawyers report.

How we defined the OPE:

1. *Each volunteer lawyer emails a monthly report with the following data points:*

   a. *The number of volunteer hours he or she anticipates for the next month*

   b. *A list of each case handled in the past month*

      i. *The number of hours the lawyer actually recorded in support of each case for the past month*

      ii. *Status/disposition of the case*

      iii. *Comment describing the outcome of each case*

2. *Availability = Actual volunteer time/Committed max volunteer time*

   a. *Actual volunteer time for the month is based on the total number of hours per case across all volunteers for the month. The EGVLP administrator adds up the number of recorded hours for each case for the month across all volunteer lawyers to get the total actual volunteer time.*

   b. *Committed max volunteer time. The EGVLP administrator adds up the anticipated monthly volunteer hours across all volunteers (from the report submitted in the preceding month).*

   c. *The result shows actual volunteer time as a percentage of time the volunteers indicate they will deliver. The EGVLP team can use this to anticipate whether recruiting is needed to bring in additional volunteers. For example, if the number of committed hours is close to what is required to support the case load, but the actual percentage delivered is significantly lower than the committed time, more volunteers may be needed, or the case load will need to be managed down.*

3. *Efficiency = Average time per client case x Number of client cases handled/Actual volunteer time*

   a. *By looking at past volunteer hours reports, the EGVLP staff determined that a client case ideally is handled within six hours of volunteer time.*

b. *Each month, the EGVLP administrator calculates efficiency by multiplying the number of cases handled as recorded by the volunteers by six hours per case and then dividing by the recorded total actual volunteer time.*

c. *If the result of this calculation is less than 80%, the team will look into whether certain cases (clients) are becoming very time intensive to take potential action to help further support the need. They can also look at whether certain volunteers, clients, or case types take longer than the average and need any special support. If the result of the efficiency calculation starts to run higher, the team may be able to accept an increase in case load.*

4. *Quality = Cases won/Total cases handled*

a. *Cases won = cases decided in favor of the client or settled successfully out of court*

b. *A low ratio of cases won may indicate a need to review case-handling processes, additional volunteer training, or even a review of the types of cases/criteria accepted into the case load.*

By implementing the OPE report, both the volunteers and the EGVLP staff will gain additional insight to increase the value of services they provide to the community.

Facilitator Kris's Journal—Elm Grove Home Weatherization Authority (EGHWA): Note 1

EGVLP referred me to an affiliate agency, the EGHWA, which offers services that insulate, rain protect, and otherwise increase energy efficiency in the home. These services are provided at no charge for low-income families in the region. Initial home evaluations are done by EGHWA staff, and the repair and installation work is handled by several home construction contractors. Because there are many vendors involved, and because the pace of work is so brisk in the fall and winter months, EGHWA experiences a large volume of incoming invoices to be paid for those services. Vendors, if they are not paid promptly, have threatened to discontinue service because this is not their most well-paying line of work.

To make the prospect of getting paid easy for these vendors, who are working for a low price, my plan is to help EGHWA increase the throughput of invoices to accelerate accurate payment. I plan to evaluate the "Table 1/Table 2" approach as a way of accelerating payment.

TABLE 1/TABLE 2—INSTANT TRIAGE OF INCOMING WORK

We are pleased to share with you a technique that has proven very useful in a number of settings where work was unevenly distributed, and projects seemingly took too long to complete. We refer to this design as Table 1/Table 2, and it works generally like this:

1. Incoming work is opened by one person known as "Table 1."

2. Table 1 sorts all this work into two groups:

   a. Simple, which is work that can be accomplished with little effort

   b. Complex, which is work that will require investigation, contact with other people, or research to resolve

3. Table 1 gives all the complex work to the other team members, known as "Table 2," so they can begin the necessary research.

4. Table 1 begins resolving all the simple work until it is complete and then joins Table 2 to help with the complex work.

Here is a variation if the simple work in this office greatly outnumbers the complex, and if Table 1 is skilled enough to handle complex work:

Points 1 and 2 are the same as above, then:

3. Table 1 passes all the simple work to Table 2, so they can resolve those items quickly. When the simple work is all complete, Table 2 assists Table 1 with the complex work.

4. Table 1 begins the research needed to resolve the complex work.

F-Note: Cross-training can be very valuable, but specializing is a fast way to get out of a crisis. Ask the team to categorize their jobs into "simple" and "complex," and then route all the simple work to one resource and all the complex to another. The time saved overall by separating these two sets of jobs is measurable and impactful.

We have deployed this technique several times. Here is one story.

"The invoices flood this place every day, especially on Fridays, and all the vendors have contracts that say they're to be paid immediately. And sometimes there is so much work that an invoice gets lost, and we have to search for it after the vendor calls our manager or the executive director."

This was the feedback from the accounts payable staff at one office we visited. Many of the invoices were easily resolved because they listed only parts and labor, the details of which were easily corroborated by reviewing the database of recent work orders. Many others, however, required validation of the contractor's completed work by an internal staff member. Frequently, a certain type of invoice would arrive with a mismatch in pricing and project number; these were habitually received from one specific vendor.

We studied the volume of each type of invoice and the time typically required to resolve it (Table 3.8).

Invoice type	Monthly volume	Resolution time
Parts and labor only	350–400 (15–20 per day)	10–15 minutes
Validation required	175–200 (9–10 per day)	25–35 minutes
Project number mismatch	35–50 (10–12 per week)	15–45 minutes

Table 3.8 Summary data from accounts payable.

We also evaluated the skill level of the staff. There were four team members, three of whom had at least two years of service, and the fourth had joined the team within the last month. We sat with them and, in a nonthreatening manner, timed their performance on a simple parts and labor invoice. We observed each of them resolving five of this type of invoice. We removed the names before sharing the data, but here in this table we will reveal for readers which of them was the newest (Table 3.9).

Team member	Shortest time	Average time	Maximum time
A	6 min	12 min	16 min
B	8 min	9.75 min	12 min
C	5 min	6.5 min	8 min
D (new)	9 min	16 min	27 min

Table 3.9 Performance data for four team members.

Based on these numbers, we built a Table 1/Table 2 model for this office that led to the efficient resolution of all invoices.

1. Table 1 was staffed by one of the A, B, or C team members and rotated each day.

2. Table 1 sorted all incoming invoices quickly into three piles:

   a. Simple — Parts and labor

   b. Complex — Validation required

   c. Complex — Project number mismatch

3. Table 1 kept the simple invoices to resolve and passed the others to Table 2.

4. Table 2, the other three team members, assigned the two complex piles as follows:

   a. One team member of A, B, or C worked on the project number mismatch category until all those invoices were resolved.

   b. The other team member of A, B, or C worked on the validation required invoice type with the assistance of team member D because contact needed to be made with several internal team members to validate the completion of work.

5. In every case, when one team member finished the work in the assigned pile, assistance was offered to the other groups.

Here is how their work was assigned (Table 3.10).

Assignment	Monday	Tuesday	Wednesday	Thursday	Friday
Triage—Simple	B	A	C	B	A
Work validation	C	B	A	C	B
Project number	A D	C D	B D	A D	C D

Table 3.10 Sample work assignment.

This table prompts two quick questions:

1. "What if someone is missing from work one day?" The answer we agreed to is that the project number category will be handled after all the work validation invoices and, if the triage—simple team member finishes first, then he or she will move to project number invoices. You and your team can agree to a plan that works for you; the important elements of this are that you:

   • Study it first and make the best plan.

   • Follow it and do not deviate until the next point below is scheduled.

   • Refine the plan periodically based on the experience of the operators.

2. "When will team member D graduate to the same level of responsibility as A, B, and C?"

Every person who joins a new organization or begins a new type of work will have some amount of learning to do before becoming fully self-sufficient. Later in Part 3, we will introduce the CASI tool, which will help team members and managers determine the level of freedom that everyone has for each type of work.

Facilitator Kris's Journal—Elm Grove Home Weatherization Authority: Note 2

We implemented the Table 1/Table 2 approach quickly with EGHWA and monitored their performance. Their rate of closing invoices for payment improved to just over half the time required before Table 1/Table 2 was deployed and, more importantly, no invoices have been lost in the shuffle of incoming work since this technique was implemented.

Lean Metrics

When you begin an improvement initiative, think for a minute about the future state. Anticipate more than just what the new process might look like by thinking of your answer to this question: "How do we know that things are better now?"

A measure of success for your project will be how you've improved the work from its previous state to the new, improved current state. The use of lean metrics like OEE will reveal the improvement and justify the time and effort that you and the project team spent to make this work simpler, smoother, more accurate, faster, and more customer friendly.

There are more metrics that can also be used to show improvement from current to future state.

1. On-time in full (OTIF). This is a measure of how many orders were fulfilled both accurately and timely. It is expressed as a percentage with a moving value from day to day or week to week, depending on the frequency of customer orders. The line chart in the upper half of the display is sufficient for tracking the organization's performance, but it is not enough if you are looking for ways to improve performance. The lower half of the display shows the number and type of defect that prevented the OTIF order during that time period.

2. Conversion rates, cost per conversion, or cost per sale for sales, including digital sales activities.

3. Metrics that are industry specific, such as emergency room patient wait times or room turnover in a medical setting, RevPAR (total revenue of hotel/total number of available rooms during measurement period) in the hotel industry, and first contact resolution (FCR) in contact centers.

What other metrics do you use to evaluate performance? We'd love to hear how you track your work. Write to us at info@flexidian.com.

Measurements—Take Out the Math

We have heard the question many times: "How should we measure our process?" It is often a response to our initial set of interview questions, which, invariably, includes, "How do you measure success?" Recall that we stress the importance of the SIPOC tool as a foundation for improvement activities and as a resource that helps answer questions just like that one.

Additionally, we often hear comments like, "We can't really measure our work because it is unique every time." There are two ways we typically handle this viewpoint:

1. Is it really unique every time? If we look closely, I think we'll find at least 50% of each transaction or project is common from one time to the next. Sure, there may be a lot of customizing or tailoring, but incremental improvements can be found throughout the process map, and we usually find a lot of common work that can be standardized or at least made a lot more consistent.

> F-Note: As a facilitator, it is critical to implement success measurements with your workshop team. This can be daunting for some. Math is not everyone's favorite subject. Having a set of simple standard and useful measurements in your toolkit will help reduce trepidation for the math adverse. Focus simply on speed and accuracy.

2. If it turns out that the projects are very different from one another, at a minimum the team can keep track of the same two basic measures that we have mentioned already in this book:

    a. Speed: How long does it take to tackle the full project and to complete every individual milestone or step along the way from start to finish? You can record this and strive to improve that speed with every new project or opportunity.

    b. Accuracy: In its most basic sense, how often was the project completed correctly on the first try? And for every step along the way: how many of those steps required rework, how much time was spent on that rework, and how many times was the project stopped and sent back for corrections?

Speed and accuracy measures can be found all over your work environment. Here are some examples we have found in our numerous projects:

Some Sample Speed Measures

- Time to first byte (TTFB) when measuring how fast a website loads

- Average speed of answer (ASA) in a contact center, which measures how fast an agent picks up a customer inquiry or the initial wait time for contact from a customer perspective

- Mean time to repair/mean time to resolve (MTTR) in any type of issue resolution scenario

- Time to close in a law firm, meaning how long it takes on average for the firm to close a file. Files kept open for longer generally involve higher legal expenses

- Speed of publication for news, journals, and other types of publications

The list goes on…

F-Note: To draw out measures in a group setting, one approach is to brainstorm metrics for speed and accuracy. Once you have the brainstormed list, have each group member put a checkmark (or a colored-dot sticker if you prefer) by three metrics in each category that he or she prefers. Take the most popular three from each category and define these metrics with the group. Discuss how each would be calculated as well as how each can be used to drive results. This discussion will typically result in the selection of the critical few metrics that can be used to drive continuous improvement.

Some Sample Accuracy Measures

- Overall accuracy
- Error rates
- Kappa coefficient
- First time resolution (FTR) in a contact center
- Cpk
- First pass yield
- Rolled throughput yield (RTY)
- Defects per unit
- DPMO

Facilitator Kris's Journal—Medic Builders (MB): Note 1

This small medical device company manufactures component parts that are used in larger assemblies produced by some of the largest medical device companies in the world. The quality of their parts is critical for patient safety and for their continued success as a supplier. Most of their parts are built with zero defects, but it seems they spend a great amount of time inspecting them for quality. They employ a small team of inspectors to ensure their parts meet the original equipment manufacturer (OEM) specifications in every batch. My contact with them was to discuss the time and expense associated with parts inspection. My tool of choice: CASI.

CASI—SPEND THE RIGHT AMOUNT OF TIME REVIEWING QUALITY

How much inspection is necessary? The answer to that question requires several bits of information. We will need to know how complex the work is, how likely a defect is, how often a defect is spotted, what the prescribed sample size is, and what our regulatory environment dictates.

We won't spend too much time on the concept of trust, because the work we do should be built as a process that can be executed by all employees, not just the ones whom you trust the most. So, in that regard, the work should ideally be designed so anyone on your staff can be trusted to complete it successfully.

As a parallel discussion, managers often delegate tasks to their team members and have not always made it perfectly clear how much authority has accompanied the assignment of the task.

There are many resources that describe a progression of freedom in the delegation of assignments. Our favorite is from the Leadershift program offered by The Oxley Group at transformingresults.com. This list is best read from the bottom to the top (Table 3.11).

4. Implement—No need to inform	Full confidence—you have proven that you can do this work, so my input is not needed, nor is it necessary for you to inform me of what action you have taken.
3. Implement and inform	I have confidence that you can handle this work, so you take action without waiting for my input. After you execute it, though, please tell me what you did so I can be sure it was done correctly. If it was not, then we will engage in damage control.
2. Consult before implementing	Now that you have handled this work with detailed instruction several times, tell me what you believe you should do to execute it instead of me telling you.
1. Wait until told	You are new, or you have had trouble with this task in the past; therefore, you will have to wait for instructions before working on this task.

Table 3.11 The four levels of freedom from Leadershift. The chart builds from the bottom upward.

Note that a team member may be at one level of freedom for a specific type of work and at another level for a different type of work. Use of the Table 1/Table 2 approach, tracking of OEE, and the CASI tool are all impacted positively by this circumstance because everyone—team members and managers alike—will know what progress is being made at all times.

The CASI tool we are introducing is a two-axis diagram (see Figure 3.3). The vertical axis is for expected quality and ranges from low expected quality at the bottom to high expected quality at the top. The horizontal axis is for level of effort that is required, also ranging from low to high.

We begin building the chart from the bottom right with the letter "I." This part of the graph is where expected quality is low, and the effort required to ensure quality is high. It is high because someone will be inspecting 100% of the output generated, so any deficiency, defect, or failure is not missed before sending it to the customer.

F-Note: It is important to express to the group that what you can EXPECT is not equal to what you WANT. For example, you may want with all your heart to win a lottery jackpot, but your rational expectation is that the odds are against you and winning is highly unlikely. Therefore, "expected quality" is the level of quality that is most likely to happen, and this is usually based on recent history and recent performance.

Recall from Part 1 that the detectability score in an FMEA reflects your ability to find a problem quickly: the low score of 1 means the defect is spotted immediately, the middle score of 3 means the defect is found later in the process but before it reaches the customer, and the high score of 9 means the defect is not discovered internally at all and is, instead, found by the customer.

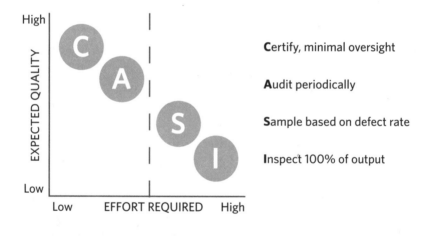

Certify, minimal oversight

Audit periodically

Sample based on defect rate

Inspect 100% of output

Figure 3.3 CASI chart to determine the level of oversight necessary to ensure top quality output.

Complexity Is a Hindrance to Quality

In multistep complex processes, errors or defects are possible with each step. The likelihood of any individual work product going through the full process without error depends on the error rate at each step. This is called rolled throughput yield (RTY), which is the probability that a process will produce a defect-free output.

Imagine a three-step process:

1. Step 1 of the process delivers an output correctly the first time 95% of the time.

2. Step 2 of the process delivers the output correctly the first time 99% of the time.

3. Step 3 of the process delivers the output correctly the first time only 85% of the time.

4. The RTY is 95% x 99% x 85% = 79.9%. This means that about 80% of the time, the output of the total process is free of defects, and about 20% of the time, the output will contain at least one defect.

With more steps in the process and more opportunities for error, the RTY decreases. For example, in a 10-step process, even with all steps performing at 99%, the RTY would only be 90.4%.

For highly complex processes with many process steps, it is best to have "drop-in" quality reviews throughout the process rather than only at the end. In this way, you can identify and remediate problem areas and increase RTY.

Let's look at two ways to deploy CASI: one with calculations and one without.

MATHEMATICAL APPLICATION OF CASI

One very useful application of the CASI tool is when there is a total number of samples that must be evaluated from the full department or team.

CASI can be very useful when you have multiple streams, operators, teams, or machines producing the work. When one of those streams is performing at a high level of quality, it should be sampled or audited less frequently than those that are performing at a lower level. Say, for instance, that your calculation calls for 170 samples per month, and you have six operators. Their defect rates are listed in Table 3.12, along with their corresponding sample frequency, as determined by using CASI. The sum of all defect rates is divided among the operators to determine a proportional rate of defect creation. Then that proportion is allocated among the 170 total required samples.

Operator	Defect rate	Proportion (of 39.1 sum)	Total samples (of 170)
1	0.054	13.8%	24
2	0.112	28.6%	49
3	0.076	19.4%	33
4	0.008	2.0%	3
5	0.051	13.0%	22
6	0.090	23.0%	39

Table 3.12 Sample: CASI determines the proportion of samples for each operator.

An example of this application of the CASI tool is in the area of quality review for documentation packets in a university enrollment department. All applications are required to have all sections of the packet completed by a certain date. The quality staff then reviews all the applications to determine whether this requirement was met. Then the quality staff's work is reviewed via audit to determine if they have evaluated the applications correctly—this is a second-level check. The regulatory oversight of university admissions is very strict about accuracy and equal opportunity. This topic was a hot story in the national news in 2019.

We calculated the overall defect rate for the entire staff's failures to discover application discrepancies, and it was low, less than 2%, meaning at least 98% of the time all discrepancies were found. We also observed that some of the quality staff were more proficient in discovering these discrepancies than others. Every month the scores are reevaluated to determine how many samples of each operator's work will be evaluated at the second level. New operators are reviewed heavily in the first month to set an initial defect rate in the table, similar to Table 3.12. The positive results of this study have been a reduction in the total number of audits required and a proportional allocation of second-level evaluations where they are needed.

SIMPLE APPLICATION OF CASI (READ: NO MATH!)

Now, we promised to extract the math from measurements and still ensure reliable evaluation even without calculations. CASI can be a very useful format for ensuring the right amount of attention is given to those who need it.

A simple Pareto chart can be used to track the frequency of certain types of errors. As described earlier, a team member may be at a higher level of freedom for one type of task than for another. Tracking errors, defects, failures, near misses, rework reasons, or other names for occurrences that were not done correctly the first time can be handled with a Pareto chart like the one shown in Figure 3.4. Simple to create, just count the number of times each type of problem arises and build the columns to a height that reflects each number. For CASI, we look at a second-level Pareto. In this example, the tallest bar is for Account#, which means the account number looked up by the call center agent was incorrect. The second-level Pareto then takes that specific problem and counts the number of times it is encountered in each area of the department. In other words, which team members experience this type of problem more than others.

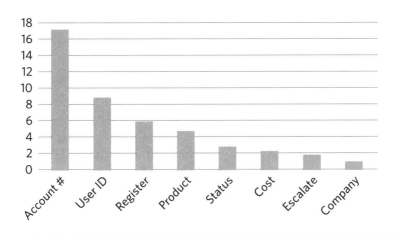

Figure 3.4 Pareto chart of errors made in a call center over two weeks.

The second-level Pareto is depicted in Figure 3.5, and it shows that Ravi had the most Account# problems over the last two weeks, followed by Sal and then Kip.

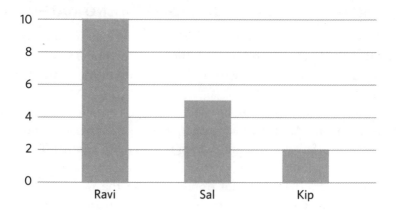

Figure 3.5 Second-level Pareto chart.

If it is important to improve the team's performance in this area, a manager will not spend an equal amount of time with each of the three team members.

Match the four levels of freedom with the CASI sequence, and you have a model for monitoring and coaching.

When someone is new or has had trouble with a particular type of task, the manager and the operator must both understand that 100% inspection will occur until performance improves. When you see that the frequency of problems is decreasing relative to the other team members or relative to historic error rates, you can move that operator to a sampling plan, which can decrease over time as performance continues to improve or which can be increased if quality begins to suffer. Level three requires only periodic audits, and full freedom is tantamount to certification in the CASI format.

We stress the importance of clearly defining which phase, which level of freedom, and which monitoring frequency each operator requires at all times.

Facilitator Kris's Journal—Medic Builders: Note 2

Quality checking at MB is less burdensome and still as accurate as it was previously, and this has enabled the team to focus on next-generation product development.

4

Meeting Facilitation
for Accountability

This Job Is Your Job

As a facilitator, you may be asked to lead meetings, workshops, or projects that are not in your primary area of responsibility. You may work in production operations and be asked to lead a project in sales operations, or you might work in the quality group and be asked to lead a workshop for the human resources department. Any practitioner of quality management, lean operations, or Six Sigma should aspire to be equally deployable to any setting and have the confidence and competence to lead that group to success.

The ASQ Six Sigma Black Belt Body of Knowledge (BoK) describes the roles that are commonly played in an improvement project. Three of these roles are process owner, project leader, and facilitator. Table 4.1 shows a comparison of those roles and responsibilities:

The main idea is that the process owner works on that job and will continue to work the job after the improvements have been identified, tested, and implemented. Indubitably, it is the process owner who must ensure the improvements stay in place after the project is complete.

The project leader executes exactly what the name of that role implies, and after the project is complete, there is no more need for that role. We have seen too many times the unfortunate spiral of a project becoming a permanent meeting. This is almost always undesirable. A project, by definition, must have a beginning and an end.

The facilitator is a role player for a specific purpose, and that is usually the fulfillment of one workshop that may involve one or many exercises the group must complete. It is possible that all three of these roles can be played by one motivated person. It is also common for a facilitator to be just what is described in Table 4.1: an invited guest who leads the workshop to completion and then departs.

Point in time	Process owner	Project leader	Facilitator
Past (before the project began)	Manages the work process that is being improved by this project or workshop	Leads the project while it is being conceived and will develop the project charter	May or may not have anything to do with the process that is being improved
Present (during the project)	Plays an important part in the project's success by defining the current state, helping identify red flags, generating new ideas, and validating process improvements	Accountable for the successful completion of the improvement project including team leadership, updates and reporting, and project closure	Plays a specific role: leading a group of people to the completion of one part of the project or execution of one tool that is identified as useful or necessary for project success
Future (after the project is complete)	Agrees to change the process and the team's behaviors based on recommendations from the project team	Discontinue this role when the project is complete	Disengage after that workshop, meeting, or session; may re-engage later, as needed

Table 4.1 Three roles compared.

With this in mind, it can be frustrating for a facilitator to be excluded from later discussions about the results of the workshop, session, or meeting that called for his or her temporary leadership. This is another undesirable circumstance. A third undesirable problem is the possibility that the project's findings will be implemented and then forgotten, and the work that was targeted for improvement will slip back to its earlier state of performance.

HANDLING QUESTIONS

It is important for workshop teams to ask questions. You will get many kinds of questions:

- Some are meant to clarify a point.
- Some are exploring the limits of the discussion.
- Some might be intended to challenge you, the facilitator.

How you handle these questions is also especially important, not just for the accuracy of the answer that is provided, but also in your ability to invite more useful questions.

Ricochet the question to the group. Allow the rest of the participants to provide responses to the question. This engages the team in the discussion and, if the question was meant to derail, the rest of the group can help you stay on track.

Boomerang the question back to the asker. Sometimes a question can be a trap, that is, the asker may be looking for you to provide a general answer for a specific situation, or the asker may have an answer in mind and is testing you to see how you respond. Return the question by saying, "How would you handle that?" or a similar volley back to the asker to uncover a useful idea he or she may have on the topic or possibly to uncover a hidden agenda.

Answer the question yourself. If you know the answer, you can provide it and move on. However, overuse of this technique can cause you to feel exposed when you do not know the answer. You can use the ricochet and boomerang techniques sometimes *even when you know the answer.*

To avoid these three undesirable conditions, we recommend setting a follow-up schedule after the completed workshop. If you are a facilitator and you lead a group of people to successful completion of one or more of the tools described in this book, for example, a game of flex hurdles, a Table 1/Table 2 assignment, or perhaps a milestone mapping exercise, set a time three, six, or nine months from now to check on that team's application of the recommendations and on their successful deployment of the prescribed process changes.

If changes have not been implemented successfully or results have not met the desired goals, you may want to offer to re-engage to facilitate another session. If the results have been successful, there may also be a need and opportunity to apply the success into another process or area of the business.

Facilitator Kris's Journal—Mullins Heating & Cooling: Follow-up visit at six months: Note 1

I had set a follow-up meeting with Mullins Heating & Cooling (from Part 1) six months after we built their action plan based on the findings of our SIPOC, FMEA, CJM, and Kano study. They showed me their metrics and described how well things were going after our earlier collaboration.

Then they asked if we could play "my worst nightmare" again for another part of their business: their 12-seat customer contact center. I had done work in many call centers in the past, so I was familiar with the common metrics and typical complaints. We set up a time to get all 12 agents together to discuss the roadblocks to productivity.

During the workshop, I learned that there are many times when the contact center agents are unclear as to what action to take based on a customer's inquiry. They said they've asked several times for guidance but cannot always get a straight answer. It is frustrating because one of their key metrics is first-contact resolution, but when they have to transfer a call or offer to call the customer back later, that metric suffers, and the customer experience can be negative.

After the workshop, I had a separate meeting with the contact center supervisor, the customer care manager, and the director of operations. They expressed frustration because the 12 agents do not always take ownership of the resolution of issues that the person on the other end of the phone, chat, or email has raised, even though they have been trained how to handle many of them.

This is a familiar story, and I told them I have a few ideas about how to help. The first is a tool I call "I-You-Who."

I-YOU-WHO—THIS JOB IS YOUR JOB

Looking back at the CASI tool we introduced in Part 3, it is possible that someone could be performing well enough in one type of work that the right level of scrutiny is *audit*, but that same person may not have achieved the same level of success with another type of work and is still at the level of *sample* for that work. This situation is common, and it can be difficult for both the operator and the supervisor to know what each is thinking unless it is documented or at least discussed. We have seen on many occasions a misunderstanding between an operator and supervisor about how much authority and accountability each of them has in the workplace. A remedy for this problem is the I-You-Who tool.

If You Can, Then You Must

There are certain responsibilities that everyone has, regardless of their length of service with the organization, their title, or their expertise. There are certain questions each person can answer and problems each person can handle. When a 16-year-old starts a new job at a banquet center and is asked by a wedding guest, "Where is the gift table?" responding with "I don't know" belongs in the category of wrong answers. "Please let me find out for you" is a much better response when the new hire is lacking the necessary information.

F-Note: The I-You-Who tool can be viewed as a simplified form of a responsibility matrix known as RACI. In a full RACI chart, the people involved in a work process are classified as responsible, accountable, consulted, or informed. While robust, it is a challenge to document with a workshop team without getting into many different perspectives of the line between responsible and accountable, who should be consulted, and other areas of argument. Taking the I-You-Who approach vastly simplifies things and achieves the desired delegation of authority and work. As the facilitator using I-You-Who, it is a good idea to remind the team to also consider who should be kept informed of workflow and decisions made.

We promote the idea that process documentation and work instructions should be written so clearly that a new hire can read, follow, and be successful *on the first day*.

I-You-Who is such a document. While it is not typically written at the keystroke level of detail, it is a thorough list of the issues an operator may encounter during a typical week (see Table 4.2).

I	YOU	WHO
Make changes to any customer contact information field in the record, except email address.	Email address changes must be referred to customer relations manager; warm transfer the call.	Any new item not already listed on this document; record new entries below for team meeting.
Overcome cancellation reasons using the guide provided by consultative sales technician.	Escalate cancellation requests to retention team via warm transfer (after using tech guide).	Customer called to ask for a rewards item that has been removed from our options; transferred to customer care.
	Lost passwords are directed to the help desk via warm transfer.	Customer requested name change without marriage or divorce decree; asked legal.
	Lost user IDs are directed to the help desk via warm transfer.	
	Requests to purchase additional products are referred to sales operations via warm transfer.	

Table 4.2 Sample I-You-Who for customer contact center operator.

Items in the first column "I" are those that the operator who owns this document must also own in action. In other words, the "I" is my responsibility. I can do it, have the authority to do it, and it must be completed by me. Failing to complete an "I" task is failing to do my job. Passing an "I" task to somebody else is shirking my responsibility. If I am found to have avoided an "I" task, there needs to be a very good reason for not completing it, or there will be consequences.

F-Note: The purpose of the I-You-Who tool is twofold: First, each operator must know who specifically can help resolve as many identifiable issues as possible, so you must ask for that list of expert resources. Second, each operator must be confident in his or her own responsibilities and must have the tools, training, and access required to resolve issues. Further, there must be no doubt that issues in the "I" column must not be passed to somebody else for resolution. You must ensure everyone is signing up for their tasks with eyes wide open.

"I" tasks generally reflect the operator's primary job description. They are the basic responsibilities that need to be carried out by the person serving in this role. Further, these "I" tasks must be handled by the operator and not sent to anybody else for action. When a team leader has to do work that the operator should be doing, it takes away productive time *from both of them.*

Send Work to the Right Place on the First Try

The "You" category is a list of tasks that must be routed to another person for action. They are either more complex, require a higher level of authority to execute, or carry some other reason for referring instead of executing them. The value of the "You" list is time savings for the operator and for the customer. Too often an operator has to ask teammates whom to ask for help with a specific type of problem. Knowing exactly who handles each specific issue saves a lot of time.

It is advisable in the "You" section to list a primary and a backup for each item if that is possible.

The "You" column is also a great source of continuous improvement opportunities—can we make a "You" item into an "I" item by simplifying the tasks involved, removing unnecessary approvals, or through other means, such as advanced training for the operator? Explore that possibility!

For efficiency, it is desirable for the I-You-Who card of the front-line operator to maximize the "I" column and continuously move work from "You" to "I."

For Anything New, Use the "Who"

If an issue arises, and it is clear who has the ability to resolve it, those issues are captured in the "I" and "You" lists described previously. If, however, an issue arises for which there is not a clear prescribed response, the "Who" category is used. In this way, the "Who" category differs from "I" and "You"—your team members will actually help to build the "Who" section as new issues arise.

The answer to a "Who" item will often be to open a help desk ticket or a request for assistance. Once the new issue has been studied and a resolution is developed, it is possible and likely that it will be moved to the "You" section, and the operator will know who to consult for help next time. It may even become an "I" issue if the operator is armed with the tools necessary to resolve it the next time it arises. This evolution from "Who" to "You" and eventually to "I" is the embodiment of empowerment for a workforce.

Facilitator Kris's Journal—Mullins Heating & Cooling Contact Center: Note 2

We brought the team of contact center agents together for a workshop on I-You-Who. As a first pass, we had each contact center agent contribute ideas on what he or she believes belongs in the "I" column and gained consensus with the group on that column. We then discussed what they thought was a "You" issue and why. For each "You" item, we documented why the team believed they were not able to resolve the listed issue. For anything they were not sure about, they entered an item in the "Who" column.

We then invited the supervisor and manager to join the workshop for a second pass. The contact center agents presented the "I" items to the supervisor and manager. In this way, the contact center agents felt ownership in claiming what was theirs to handle. This can be more effective than being handed a list of responsibilities by the supervisor or manager.

For the "You" column, having the reason each item was placed in this column on first pass was critical in setting the tone of the conversation as one of seeking resolution and alignment rather than one of not taking ownership. The agents explained to the supervisor and manager what would be needed for them to take ownership of each task. The supervisor and manager were surprised to discover that with a few small changes and clear permission granted, the agents were able to move several items from the "You" to the "I" column. One example was being able to refund the cost of certain service visits within defined parameters to resolve issues without having to escalate to the supervisor for a signature. The supervisor and manager agreed to work with the director on the remaining "You" columns to set a plan for future continuous improvement to further empower the staff.

For the "Who" column, the team was able to resolve most of the items in the list into the "You" or "I" columns, and the supervisor and manager had a clearer picture of some of the issues facing their front-line staff.

The team also agreed to use the I-You-Who card as a standing team meeting agenda item moving forward. During each team meeting, the agents will bring forward new issues or questions that have arisen in the "Who" column and collaborate with the supervisor to determine if the given item belongs in "I" or "You." The supervisor and manager committed to continuing to remove obstacles to empower the agents to take on more from the "You" column.

Facilitator Kris's Journal—Mullins Heating & Cooling Contact Center: Note 3

After 60 days, I checked back again to Mullins to see how the contact center is doing. This time I did it with a virtual meeting instead of going on-site.

The I-You-Who tool has been well-received and is now being built for all operators across the business with the contact center leading the way.

The problem now being discussed is that nothing ever seems to come from many of the team meetings that are scheduled during the week at Mullins. Meetings take place, people arrive late, people leave early, and at the next meeting it's like starting all over again.

There is a very lean tool I use called "half-life follow-up" that will be helpful for Mullins to address the issue of meeting follow-up.

HALF-LIFE FOLLOW-UP—SO THERE IS
NO DOUBT ABOUT WHAT NEEDS TO BE DONE

How many times have you concluded a meeting thinking everyone was clear about what needed to be done, but when you meet the next time no one has accomplished anything? Following are some common responses to your question of "Why not?"

"I didn't think we agreed that I was going to do that."

"I thought you were going to do that."

"I ran out of time and couldn't get to it."

"That assignment was too much to get done."

How can you prevent this frustrating problem? There are many interventions prescribed in the pages of a bookstore's business section. One technique we have found very useful is half-life follow-up.

We tip our cap to the visionary coaching expertise of The Oxley Group, where their half-life of coaching[14] principle has been shared and promoted for many years. The tool is described by Oxley in organizational development and personnel management environments as cutting the normal time for follow-up in half to prevent the condition where, for example, you set a development goal, and 30 days later you meet again and nothing has happened. A scheduled meeting after 15 days to check progress can reinforce the need to be ready at the 30-day mark.

Our deployment of half-life follow-up is typically tied more to projects and workshops than to personal development. During a kaizen workshop, there are many things that are within the project team's control and can be changed before adjourning and going back to work, especially if the meeting was scoped well and the attendees include those who have the authority to ratify process and policy changes. There will, however, often be items that require follow-up after the workshop. Letting those follow-up items drop to the floor without action is a great source of frustration as well as an obstacle to full implementation of the project's prescribed improvement actions.

---

[14] https://www.transformingresults.com/the-half-life-of-coaching/

F-Note: If everyone leaves the meeting and no one has recorded the necessary follow-up steps, it is possible, indeed probable, that many of the decisions made during the meeting will not be realized. An action register is explained later in Part 4, and you as the facilitator must ensure these actions are completed.

At the close of a kaizen workshop, there are usually three groups of action items:

1. Those that are changed during the meeting and will now be executed.

2. Those that require a bit more time and effort before they can be executed.

3. Those that are not possible to schedule under current conditions—more of a wish list.

The first group of actions is triumphant because we have actually made those changes, and the team has agreed to use the new procedures starting right now. We will use the ongoing data collection discussed previously.

The third group is often frustrating because we can't make those changes now. Action items might be on that list because they would require a change that is too expensive, they might not be manageable with the current computer system, or some other reason. At least we can say it is better to know what cannot be done—and why—than to remain uninformed.

The list we are most concerned about is the second—those items that we believe we can implement but not right now while we are in the kaizen workshop. There could be several reasons why an action would be listed in this category, for example:

• Another department, functional area, or work unit that is not represented in this kaizen workshop needs to be consulted prior to implementation.

• A change that was not able to be tested during the kaizen workshop must still be tested prior to implementation.

- A change requires some technical development effort.
- A change requires funding that needs to be validated before going forward.
- A change requires training and/or change management to be developed and implemented.

When we review this list and prepare the action register that is described later in this part, we usually allow two possible responses from those who volunteer to own each item:

1. You can schedule the next step for completion *next Friday*, or

2. You can schedule the next step for completion *the following Friday!*

We do not want action items sitting on a list and making no progress.

The half-life follow-up tool is easy to describe and deploy. If there is an action item that is scheduled for completion in 10 days, you as the facilitator will check with the owner of that task after five days. If the progress being made demonstrates that the action owner will successfully complete the item in time for the 10-day deadline, there is no further need to check on it. However, if progress is insufficient or unconvincing, you and the action owner review the item and its importance, and you reinforce the need to complete it at the 10-day mark.

Then, after cutting the original allotted time in half (due in 10 days = review in five days), you now check with the action owner again in half the remaining time (due in five more days = review again in about two days). If progress is still not certain, you will check again in another day.

In theory, you are cutting the remaining time in half at every check point, so you could actually be pestering the action owner two hours before the follow-up meeting, and then one hour before, and then half an hour before, etc. In practice, these intervals should really not be needed for most action items.

F-Note: As a meeting facilitator, additional tactics to incorporate to help make meetings more impactful include:

- Provide an agenda and stick to it during the meeting. This will ensure meetings are focused and results-oriented on the intended topics.
- Make a list of topics and questions that arise that should be addressed later by the group. This "parking lot" approach helps people keep on agenda.
- Communicate ground rules, such as meetings start and stop on time, no interrupting each other, no side discussions, and silence is considered consent. Hold participants to the rules.
- Become familiar with techniques, such as round-robin and nominal group technique, that can ensure no one monopolizes the conversation and everyone is able to contribute.
- Ensure consensus is achieved. All participants must act as a united front to support the decision.
- Document all actions in an action register (addressed further in this part).
- At the end of the meeting, review action assignments and establish the time for the next meeting.

We can think of times when such detailed follow-up might actually be needed, though. If you are watching to see a new software change that is going live, you might want to check on a half-life follow-up schedule to make sure everything is going smoothly and that the move-up will be successful.

We have found that many action items only reach the top of someone's priority list when they see the due date looming shortly on their calendar, often that same day. By deploying a half-life project management approach, you keep the action item front of mind for the action owner and reduce the likelihood of reaching the due date without action being taken.

WHAT'S IN MY VIRTUAL FACILITATOR BAG?

Virtual meetings may be a more cost-effective and efficient means of following up than going on-site. As a facilitator, you may find yourself running full workshops virtually or with a mix of in-person and virtual attendees as teams are often not co-located. There are many free and/or cost-effective tools that enhance digital facilitation. Some options we like include:

- Virtual sticky notes and whiteboards through apps such as Stormboard

- Videoconferencing including inexpensive options such as Skype, Zoom, and Google Hangouts

- Online collaboration in Slack, Yammer, and similar options

- Surveying tools include SurveyMonkey and Google Forms

- File storage and sharing through DropBox (up to 2GB free), Google Drive (15GB), and OneDrive (5GB)

There are many other options as well—this is just to name a few to get you started on exploring leveraging digital tools for productive workshops and meeting facilitation. Being well-prepared and versatile is critical for any successful facilitation, whether in-person or virtual.

Facilitator Kris's Journal—Mullins Heating & Cooling Contact Center: Note 4

I usually start an introductory meeting with a team of operators by asking something like, "If we can find ways to save 10% of your time at work, to give you back three to four hours each week, what would you do with all that time?" When we met about the I-You-Who tool and half-life follow-up, I focused on the specific problems they raised and not on a general approach to saving time. I have another chance now to reach this group on a more general level of lean. I want to help them approach their day-to-day responsibilities in a way that only the essentials are done and the extraneous is avoided. The tool I'll introduce them to is flex RM.

FLEX RM TOOL—A PERIODIC CLEANOUT
OF UNNECESSARY OBLIGATIONS

Agent A: "I'd like to help you with your problem, but I have to get this report done by noon."

Agent B: "Really? Who reads that report?"

A: "I don't really know anymore. I have a pretty long distribution list."

B: "Well, when was the last time someone asked you about it after you sent it?"

A: "Ask me about it?! No, no one ever asks me anything about the report."

And the questions can continue:

"How long have you been building this report?" Too long.

"How many new additions have been requested for this report?" Lots of them, all the time.

"How much interpretation do you provide when building the report?" None, really. It's mainly collecting data points and retyping them.

And our favorite question: "Did you ever NOT send the report just to see who calls you to ask about it?" No, but I will now!

We applaud this line of questioning.

HISTORY: THE RAMMPP MATRIX

One useful tool that was used widely at General Electric in the 1980s was the RAMMPP matrix. The tool's purpose was to remove unnecessary work, much like lean theory, but the approach was even simpler. Teams were asked to list the reports, approvals, meetings, metrics, policies, and procedures they faced during their daily work. Then the list of questions below was used to evaluate each item on the list. Often the time saved in a work week was surprisingly large, as much as three or four hours per week.

In fact, there is a tool we use called flex RM that includes questions similar to these and is used for the purpose of removing unnecessary reports from your work routine. Flex RM is a more concise version of an old, trusted waste reduction tool called the RAMMPP matrix. In fact, the "RM" in flex RM refers to reports and meetings, a subset of the targets from the older technique.

As a facilitator, you are expected to bring a fresh perspective to the work environment that you've been asked to improve or streamline. So, your questions are welcome, but they need to be well-directed.

Ask the group to take a little time and list all the reports they generate. This list should include the reports that each individual creates and also a separate list of reports that two or more members of the group collaborate to build and share. The two lists should not include any repeated reports; every report should be listed only once on the full document.

Next, ask the group to list all the meetings they attend on a regular basis. This will often include weekly team meetings, daily huddles, project team meetings, update meetings, and more. Again, there will be two parts to the list: those meetings that each individual attends, and a separate list for meetings where two or more members of the team participate. Each unique meeting should be listed only once when the list is complete. It can be very surprising to look at the long list of meetings once it has been built.

F-Note: One quick way to start building a list of meetings is to check the online calendar used by each team member.

Now that both lists, the "R" for reports and the "M" for meetings, have been built for individuals and for the team, you have a very powerful list of questions to ask. Begin at the top of this question list. If the answer is "No," then proceed through the remaining questions until the answer is "Yes."

Flex RM Questions

1. Can it (the report or the meeting) be eliminated?

2. Can it be partially eliminated?

3. Can it be done less often?

4. Can it be delegated to somebody else?

5. Can it be done using a more productive technology?

6. Can it otherwise be simplified?

Let's look at these questions one at a time.

1. *Can it be eliminated?*

   You are asking the group an important question, but it's possible they may not have the authority to answer it. The underlying question for this group—the people who generate the report in question and the people who attend the meeting you're asking about—is "what is the risk of not doing it anymore?" They will have insight regarding this question, and they may be very motivated to stop producing this report or to stop attending this meeting. You must realize that a higher level of approval may be required to answer this question in the affirmative.

2. *Can it be partially eliminated?*

   We have found, and perhaps you have also seen, that reports rarely get shorter, but they often get longer. More bits of information are requested, or managers send messages like: "Could you add another view of the analysis to this report?"

   > *F-Note:* When validating whether a report is still necessary, you must not ask, "Do you still need this report?" because the answer will almost always be, "Yes!" and then the conversation has ended, and you may lose your chance to change.

   In several kaizen events we have asked the consumers of regular reports this question: "Which parts of the report are most important to you?" When the response is something like, "I only read the executive summary," or "I skip right to the graphs on page 12," then you may have the opportunity to reduce the size of the final report and, as a result, to decrease the amount of time and effort you expend in producing it.

   Partially eliminating a report or meeting means doing only the right amount of work: building only the essentials into the report, posting the report in one central location instead of emailing it to individuals, and attending meetings with a clear agenda that is followed diligently so it may not actually have to last for the hour that was scheduled.

3. *Can it be done less often?*

   Meetings that happen every week are sometimes necessary if the pace of change in the matter being discussed is that frequent. We have also seen meetings scheduled on a weekly basis and then canceled at the last minute if there is nothing to share. However, the time that has been reserved on each person's calendar seemed like it was committed, and this may have prevented them from scheduling something else during that time. Sending a

> **F-Note:** When storing reports to a centralized location, use a naming convention that includes the date of the report in the name of the file. Consider keeping only the most current report in the main location and moving the others to an archive. This will reduce the risk of someone making decisions using outdated information.

report every week or with a frequency that is more often than the consumers of that report can even read it is also a waste. Decreasing the update and delivery rate of a report can save you time. Additionally, posting the report to a central location and giving consumers of that information access to the report's shared location will save you effort in distributing the report, as we discussed in the 5S section in Part 3.

4. *Can it be delegated to somebody else?*
While this question may seem like shuffling unnecessary work to somebody else instead of reducing or eliminating it, remember that we have already asked questions 1, 2, and 3, and the answer to these was "No." It is possible that someone else may be better positioned to generate the information needed for the report we are discussing, and that someone else may be more suited to attend the meeting we are discussing. If participation in the meeting amounts to taking notes and bringing information back to the team, or if input from your team needs to be brought to the meeting and shared with the meeting participants, that is different than sending a participant to a meeting where decisions need to be made or discussions will take place that require judgment or valuable input from your team's representative.

5. *Can it be done using a more productive technology?*
For meetings that still need to happen, you can ask the team whether they might be able to make changes that will make

participation more efficient. As mentioned previously, if input is required from your team, why not send that information to the other meeting participants in advance using an online collaboration tool? Or, it might also be possible to conduct voting using an online survey tool instead of needing to vote concurrently during the meeting.

6. *Can it otherwise be simplified?*
The tools and techniques shared through lean thinking include additional ways to streamline work when the work being done is viewed as a process—a series of steps taken to transform inputs into valuable outputs.

Facilitator Kris's Journal—Mullins Heating & Cooling Contact Center: Note 5

It's been quite productive working with the Mullins contact center team and wonderful to see them lead the way in sharing these tools and techniques across the organization. They've eliminated unnecessary meetings, implemented a meeting process to ensure that when there is a meeting it is effective, simplified reports to focus on sharing what is critical to the business, and established clear documentation on ownership of issue resolution.

The team supervisor has developed her facilitation expertise along the way as well! One final critical tool I will leave them with is the action register. Creating and maintaining an action register is a simple way to manage all the actions coming out of workshops and meetings.

ACTION REGISTER

The action register is a critical output of any workshop or meeting. It lists the agreed-upon actions, owners, timeline, and next steps from which the project leader and process owners can manage and complete follow-up.

The facilitator brings the action register template into the meeting or workshop (see Table 4.3).

Agreed action	Primary owner	Action type	Next step	Due date of next step	Completion target
Short description of the improvement to be implemented	Single person accountable to make sure the action is completed	Is it a quick win, project, etc. (see list below)	Describe the next thing to be done to make progress	Near-term date next step will be completed	Target date to complete all steps/final implementation

Table 4.3 Action register.

In the action type column in Table 4.3, the following options are suggested:

- **Quick win (or do it now)** — Something that can be achieved that day or very shortly after with a minimal number of steps by the owner. It does not require further approvals or discussion. The owner just needs to get it done.

- **Start a project** — Something the team has approved/agreed to complete but will involve a more complex set of steps or interdependencies. The owner needs to draft and then work through a project plan to accomplish the desired end result.

- **Approval needed (or negotiate)** — Before moving forward, someone who was not in the meeting needs to approve the effort. The owner's next step is typically to gain the necessary approval. Once approved, the "type" column should then be updated to reflect quick win, start a project, etc.

- **Research (or study further)** — The team in the meeting did not have enough data to make a firm decision. More information is needed. The owner will look into it further and bring data back to the team to make a decision.

- **Consider for the future** — There may be actions the team would like to take, but timing is not right to pursue it currently for a variety of business reasons. It's good to track such actions and even assign an owner. The owner will be periodically reminded of the action and is responsible to bring it forward to the team for consideration again when the time is more ideal.

- **Do not pursue** — It may also be useful to track actions that were considered and rejected/decided against. For these, in place of a "next step," consider including a brief statement of why the decision not to pursue was made. If the decision factors change in the future, a "do not pursue" item might be more viable to consider. Additionally, it is sometimes helpful to report what the team decided not to pursue and why.

Some teams may opt to use additional action types, such as automate, DMAIC project, pilot test, or lean opportunity. Use a standard set of action types that work well for your business. The important thing is that all team members understand what each action type means and labels them consistently.

A strong note-taker (or facilitator who is also taking notes) can draft the agreed action column during the meeting, capturing all the actions that need to take place. The facilitator plans time at the end of the meeting to walk through the captured agreed actions, gain alignment from the meeting attendees, and complete the remaining columns.

F-Note: A good practice is to allow about 12% of your meeting time for the action register to close out the meeting. That works out to about seven to eight minutes for a one-hour meeting, 14 to 15 minutes for a two-hour meeting, about 30 minutes for a four-hour effort, and approximately the final hour for a full-day workshop.

In follow-up meetings and conversations, the action register is then updated to track completed and new "next steps" for each action until the improvement effort is completed. New actions for the same effort may be added into the register in follow-up meetings as needed. The action register from a workshop can and should be used to form the agenda for follow-up meetings.

Case Study

Let's see how our intrepid facilitator, Kris, can put these tools to use.

First up, the Radisonville School District (RSD). Kris got a call from the superintendent of RSD in April, close to the end of the school year, asking whether the projects that have been so successful for the city can be replicated for the school district. Ever the optimist, Kris replied that yes, many of the tools and techniques that have helped the city can be applied in any situation. "Well," said the superintendent, "let's start with a pretty big problem we have at Radisonville High School and see what we can do."

THE PAIN

During the first month of school, the front desk at Radisonville High School (RHS) is usually inundated with phone calls and emails from parents expressing problems with registration, enrollment, schedules, bus routes, dietary restrictions, sports physicals, and more. The front desk staff of three full-time administrative specialists and a part-time administrative assistant are overwhelmed by calls and notes. This is compounded by the walk-in questions that students have, many of which are on those same topics. The problem is that the month of September is a critical time for arranging state-mandated testing, and these other issues present prioritization challenges for the office staff. The principal at RHS would like the staff to be able to handle the full workload, including problem resolution and testing arrangements.

Kris suggested a scoping meeting and was able to meet with the superintendent and the principal to decide on an approach. They developed a list of critical success factors (CSFs), which is key for any process improvement initiative. The CSFs describe the desired outcomes of the process in question. They named the project, "Reduce first-month admin burden on RHS front desk staff," and their list of CSFs is shown in Table C.1.

Critical Success Factors		
For the student	**For the school**	**For regulators**
Fast resolution of problems	Maximum efficiency for each type of problem	State tests arranged compliant with time requirements
Meet graduation requirements	Utilize existing technology to assist with completion of tasks	
Meet sports participation requirements		
Stress-free entry into the new school year		

Table C.1 Critical success factors for the RHS front desk project.

Notice that the CSF list in Table C.1 is divided into three categories. CSFs should reflect the needs of:

1. Your customer

2. Your organization

3. All regulatory authorities

SIPOC: THE FIRST STEP TOWARD PROCESS AND DATA ANALYSIS

Admittedly, Kris had not worked in a school setting before this project and was feeling a bit apprehensive. However, experience has shown that the quality and innovation tools we have shared in this book are trustworthy. Now that the first step had been taken—

building the list of CSFs—the next step was to create the SIPOC for the front-desk team's work.

Kris gathered the team after school one day and asked them to describe at a high level their activities during the first month of school, way back in September. Most of the team had been with the school for several years, so recalling September was not difficult. They listed these six main functions:

1. Help students find locations.
2. Diagnose transportation problems.
3. Schedule state tests.
4. Schedule sports physicals.
5. Update student records.
6. Route other issues to the right person.

F-Note: Notice this list of six items is not really sequential. This is an acceptable adaptation of SIPOC, an important goal of which is to list the inputs and outputs.

Next Kris asked the team, "What are the desired outputs for each of those items?" and then, "What are the undesired outputs of those items?" emphasizing that it is important to understand what we are trying to produce and what we are trying to avoid to improve the work we are doing. The SIPOC in Table C.2 shows the results of this meeting.

Questioning continued by asking for the customer of each output, the inputs required to complete each of the six functions, and the sources for each of those inputs.

One thing they learned by building the SIPOC is that there are some similarities in the inputs required for the six functions, and they could save some effort by reusing those bits of information.

F-Note: Recall that the outputs column of a SIPOC is not just a place to list the results of the process. It is important to know whether success was achieved and, in the case of non-success (failure!), the reasons for that failure. Undesired outcomes are just as important to track as the desired results.

Further, they realized that there are a few functions that everyone needs to know how to do, but others can be handled by one or two team members because they are less frequent and require specialized knowledge. This topic is addressed below in the Table 1/Table 2 conversation.

Sources	Inputs	Process/ Function	Outputs (measurable)	Customers
• TTY* system	• Student's schedule	• Help students find locations	• # of lost or absent students	• Teachers and students
• TTY • Bus route database	• Master bus schedules	• Diagnose transportation problems	• # of missed buses • # of bus complaints	• Drivers, parents, students
• TTY • State database	• Test schedule, student's schedule	• Schedule state tests	• # of schedule changes • # of schedule conflicts open and resolved	• Students, parents, state reporting agent
• Master sports schedule • TTY	• Reporting dates, student's schedule	• Schedule sports physicals	• # of proactive rescheds • # of reactive rescheds	• Coaches, students
• TTY • RSD/RHS master database	• Student's schedule, master class list	• Update student records	• # of problems resolved • # of problems not accurately identified	• Students, counselors
• Various	• TBD	• Route other issues to the right person	• # and category of known and new issues raised	• Students, others

Table C.2 SIPOC for the front-desk project at RHS.

TTY: fictional database of all student records

The next day Kris met with the principal and explained that a good improvement project follows both the data analysis path and the process analysis path. In building the SIPOC, they set the stage for both of these paths. The next steps will be to initiate data analysis with a Pareto chart of the issues that arose last September and to study the process for getting the work done by interviewing the team members in more detail than is depicted in the SIPOC. The principal agreed and gave Kris access to last year's data and permission to set up meetings with the staff for interviews.

PARETO ANALYSIS

The previous year's notes were helpful in prioritizing the issues that needed the most attention to save the front desk staff the most time next September. Kris reviewed the notes and built a Pareto chart of the issues raised during the first month of the school year. Figure C.1 shows that Pareto chart.

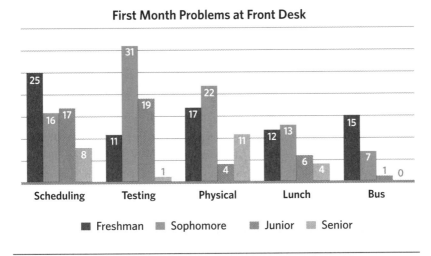

First Month Problems at Front Desk

Figure C.1 Pareto/Paynter chart for first-month issues. See the following F-Note.

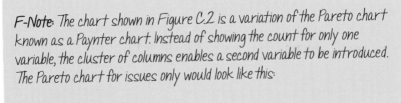

F-Note: The chart shown in Figure C.2 is a variation of the Pareto chart known as a Paynter chart. Instead of showing the count for only one variable, the cluster of columns enables a second variable to be introduced. The Pareto chart for issues only would look like this:

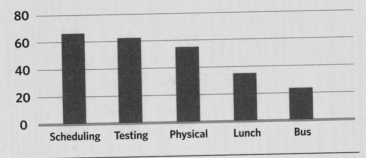

Figure C.2 Pareto chart for first-month issues only.

Adding the grade level for each student's issue helps to identify in more detail where these problems are occurring. You can see, for instance, that state testing is a significant issue, but it is mainly causing problems for sophomores, while seniors have almost no trouble in that area.

The Pareto chart revealed that scheduling, state testing, and sports physicals were the more frequently occurring types of issues that the front desk team had to resolve, although it seemed during conversation that bus issues were the biggest problem. The reason for this was discovered in the team meeting when Kris presented the Pareto chart of last year's problems. Although bus problems were the fewest, they often required the most effort to resolve. Rerouting a bus is not something the front desk staff or even RSD can control; the bus routes are determined centrally at the RSD offices.

It is important not only to measure the frequency of occurrence when tracking problems and creating a Pareto chart, but it is also important to understand the severity or impact of each type of problem. If the list from last year had included the number of times there was a specific type of problem, as well as how long it took to resolve each one, the list might have looked like Table C.3 and been more useful in preparing the next steps in process and data analysis.

Date	Issue raised	Time	Comments
Aug. 22	Bus route missed—Spring St. at Main St.	45 min	Rerouted #107 to that site
Aug. 22	Change math 143 to math 144 for L. Jacobie (soph)	4 min	Updated in TTY
Aug. 23	Bus route missed—Glade St. at Ridge Park Dr.	72 min	Reassigned to bus #60
Aug. 24	Lunch items not located—dietary	2 min	Salad bar location specified
...	...	...	...
Sept. 16	Soccer physical missed by D. Dawssen (fresh)	8 min	Rescheduled to Sept. 18

Table C.3 Abbreviated list of issues handled by front desk staff including time required to resolve.

A problem with this, of course, is that it takes an extra minute to track the activity that was just completed. It is sometimes easy and sometimes heroic to resolve a student's (or a customer's) issue successfully. It is always regarded as a burden to record the action that was just taken. However, without those important bits of data, the organizational knowledge is lost, and that problem will persist. The purpose of a Pareto analysis is to:

1. Identify an issue.
2. Evaluate its magnitude in terms of frequency and/or severity.
3. Solve the issue:
   a. First, learn how to solve it no matter what it takes.
   b. Next, learn how to solve it right the first time.
   c. Then, learn how to solve it as quickly as possible.
4. Ideally, find ways to eliminate the problem in the first place.

Pointing to the fourth item on this list of issues, Kris asked the team, "What would it take to make lunch item identification disappear as a problem?" A few ideas emerged, and three of them seemed to make the most sense during the discussion:

1. Post more visible, colorful signs in the lunchroom just above average head height describing the food offerings and indicating with arrows what is served at each location.

2. Orient the students during the first-day tours to the setup of the lunchroom.

3. Appoint a motivated "barker" (like a circus announcer: "Hurry, Hurry, Step Right Up!) at the front entrance to the lunchroom and another at the side entrance announcing statements like "Today's special at the grill line is meatloaf," or "Salad bar with healthy options is near the stage."

While the initial signs described in solution #1 above were made of poster board and markers, the suggestion was made to install electronic video boards so the specific menu items could easily be changed every day.

PILOT TESTING YOUR SOLUTIONS

Several of the solutions that were generated during the RHS study were able to be tested late in the school year, so they could be validated as improvements and fine-tuned as necessary before the start of the next school year.

The lunchroom solutions were tested in May and were very successful in minimizing the number of questions the front desk staff had to handle regarding dietary needs. However, it is unclear whether the lack of questions reflected the depth into the school year, that is, by the month of May students have likely learned their way around the lunchroom. To gather more information, the project team surveyed the students about the usefulness of the signs and the barkers and, while they expressed a little hesitation with the loudness of the student barkers, they thought the idea was helpful, and also that the signs were visible and useful.

PRIORITIZATION FOR ACTION

To handle a high volume of transactions in any department, especially during a time of work overload, a very useful technique we described in Part 3 of this book is Table 1/Table 2. In this model, one person initially screens incoming work and decides whether he or she will handle it individually or send it to another person. Common models were shared in Part 3, but there are typically two options:

1. The sorter moves all easy work to Table 2, so the person at Table 2 can quickly resolve those simple issues without getting bogged down by one or more complex issues. The sorter at Table 1 begins to handle all the complex issues individually until Table 2 finishes the simple tasks and then joins the pursuit of resolution for the complex issues.

2. The sorter moves all complex work to Table 2 and begins to handle all the simple tasks until those are complete. This is a reversal of option #1 above.

At RHS, the Pareto study revealed that bus issues were decidedly more complex and took a longer time to resolve. With that in mind, the team of three full-time administrative specialists and one part-time administrative assistant agreed that the bus problems should be routed to one of them for handling, rather than taking the chance that more than one bus problem would arise at the same time and result in multiple front-desk team members working on a complex bus issue at the same time. Such a situation could limit their ability to respond to the needs of other students and adults who walked into the front desk space to ask for help. Diane, a member of the front desk team for 11 years who was very familiar with the process for defining bus routes, was selected as the captain of bus route resolution.

Further, the scheduling of state testing was assigned to Pat, who had the most experience in this area.

This diagram in Figure C.3 was drawn by Kris and the project team on a whiteboard, and it became their test model for the remainder of this school year:

Table 1/Table 2 Plan

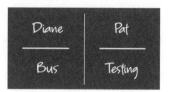

Table 1: Handle as raised

Table 2: Route complex issues

Figure C.3 Table 1/Table 2.

EVOLUTION AND DELEGATION

Of the three full-time administrative specialists who work at the front desk in RHS, two have worked there for more than 10 years, and the third was just hired at the beginning of last year. The pressure of a new school year was handled by the junior administrative specialist with a smile, but later it was shared that he often felt overwhelmed and didn't feel comfortable asking questions of the others while they were busy helping people.

The tool we introduced to help members of the team know how to handle the situations they are likely to face is I-You-Who, described in detail in Part 4.

For Tom, the junior administrative specialist at RHS, the simplest issues to resolve were lunch and schedule, because he proactively became familiar with the layout of the lunchroom before the school year began, and because the TTY system was very intuitive, and he was instructed thoroughly during his own new hire orientation. Issues related to buses, state tests, sports physicals, and other problems were not as easy for him to resolve.

Kris led a separate session with the project team where they built an I-You-Who for Tom. It is shown in Table C.4.

I own and resolve	Transfer to (you)	Who can respond?
Lunch/dietary issues	Bus routes—refer to Diane	
Student schedule changes	State testing changes—refer to Pat	
	Broken laptop—refer to Kelly in Technology	
	Police request—refer to Principal Davis	
	Band question—contact Mrs. Taylor in band	
	Immigration form—contact counselor Ghavi	

Table C.4 I-You-Who for front desk staff, specifically built for Tom, the junior member of the team.

While the list of referrals and contacts may seem quite long at times, it is helpful for Tom and others to know who can answer a specific question to save time for the customer and to get the correct answer on the first try.

F-Note: For I-You-Who to be used effectively, two important elements must be practiced:

1. It must be updated every time a referral resource changes. Good guidance is also to open the I-You-Who list once per month to see if any names need to be changed.

2. You must ask the right questions to correctly diagnose the problem. Just because someone uses the word "band" in the question does not necessarily mean it is a band issue. It could be, "I am in the band, how can I still catch the right bus?"

The team built the I-You-Who and put a copy on each cube in the front desk area. No matter who was responding to an issue, it was easy to see who was best suited or designated to resolve a certain type of issue.

Recall that the third column in I-You-Who is for unknown issues that need support from someone not named in the you column. During the first month of a new school year, a problem could arise that no one has heard before. Going back to our discussion on data collection for a Pareto analysis, the amount of extra time that is needed to record an issue on a data collection sheet is worth the trouble, because we will use those bits of information to make lasting, positive improvements quickly. *Without data, improvements are simply good luck.*

ANTICIPATING QUESTIONS—AND ANSWERS

One type of issue faced by the front desk team was not always predictable. This was the area of sports physicals, and it was because there are many exceptions to the stated rules. While the deadlines for sports physicals were detailed in the guidance provided by the state's office of education standards, acceptable modifications were based, in part, on the opinions of the myriad doctors around the state whose patients are students at RHS and other schools. In other words, interpretation of the rules was inconsistent from district to district. RSD strove to standardize the approach to sports physicals, but the law was not always clear.

F-Note: Remember the story of the Japanese white gloves. Rules must be enforced, or they are not valuable. And those rules must be enforced firmly and politely in order to ensure compliance. No one must be able to say, "I got an exception."

To maintain consistency from student to student and from year to year, the state's rules were shared with parents along with an FAQ list that outlined some common exceptions. In addition to those stated exceptions, a response router was provided to the front desk staff with the answers to some more questions that have been raised in recent years. The response router presents the opportunity to improve results in both speed and accuracy. It is a time saver when searching for the right answer, and it ensures anyone answering the question will provide a consistent response.

KRIS'S ROADMAP

1. CSFs to guide the project team
2. SIPOC to identify inputs and outputs
3. Pareto/Paynter to quantify the problems
4. Table1/Table2 to triage incoming work and optimize workload
5. I-You-Who to route issues to the right person
6. Response router to anticipate problems and answer them quickly
7. Action register to organize follow-up

Appendix
16 Facilitator Tool Guides

The following pages provide single-sheet summary construction guides of each of the 17* facilitator tools covered throughout this book. These are for quick reference as you facilitate meetings and workshops.

These tools are all available for viewing or printing at our website: http://www.flexidian.com

Two tools are combined as Tool 6

TOOL 1: SIPOC
flexidian.com/sipoc

Ask the project team these questions:

1. What are we mapping?

   a. Remind the group that we are mapping the way this work is being done today, not in the future or in a dream state of perfection.

   b. Title the SIPOC at the top with a description of the work being done and today's date.

Completing the Process section

We recommend bracketing the process section with the starting and ending points of the job first so the team doesn't create a long, rolling list of process steps. Achieving a succinct list of four to seven high-level steps is easier when filling in the links between the trigger and the conclusion.

2. What is the first step we do to complete this work? This can also be asked as: What is the trigger that initiates this work?

3. What is the last step: When is the work complete?

4. Now let's fill in the high-level steps in between:

   a. Build each box as VERB-OBJECT.

   b. Limit it to no more than seven boxes.

Completing the Outputs section

5. What are the desired outputs of this work?

6. What are the undesirable or unfortunate outputs of this work today?

7. Now, how do we measure each of those outputs? In other words, how do we know we did a good job?

   a. Speed: How long does each one take to produce or how timely is it delivered?

   b. Accuracy: How well does each one meet the customer's requirements, or how often does each undesirable output occur?

Adding the Customers section

8. Who is the customer for each output?

Completing the Inputs section

9. Now, to the inputs column—what do we need to execute step 1?

   a. Look for tools, materials, information, and anything else that is needed to accomplish that process step.

   b. Repeat for each step.

   c. The group can decide whether to repeat inputs that are used in multiple steps.

10. How do we measure these inputs?

   a. This may include speed and accuracy measures.

   b. It may also involve sorting and listing the possible variations of each input.

Adding the Sources section

11. What are the sources for each input?

TOOL 2: MY WORST NIGHTMARE
flexidian.com/my-worst-nightmare

1. Ask each participant to post sticky notes (virtually or in person) to a whiteboard or flip chart describing the worst possible outcomes of the project or improvement that is to be implemented.

2. After all the ideas are collected, read each submitted item out loud for all to hear. Keep the ideas anonymous—the facilitator should read all the ideas without asking for any feedback or comments on who submitted what.

3. Ask the group a series of debrief questions:

   a. Which ideas surprised you?

   b. What images did these ideas conjure in your mind?

   c. Which of them are more likely to actually happen?

   d. What can we do to prevent them?

4. For any collected ideas, be sure to document those that are likely to actually happen, as well as ideas around how to prevent them from occurring. You can explore these further using FMEA (see Tool 3).

TOOL 3: FLEX FMEA
flexidian.com/flex-fmea

To create the flex FMEA, first generate a list of what could go wrong; a good starting point can be found using the SIPOC and my worst nightmare (MWN) results if you have already completed those exercises.

1. Create a table with five columns labeled:

Potential issue	If it happens, how severe is the impact to the customer? [SEV]	How likely is this to occur, or how often has it occurred? [OCC]	How easy is it to detect this issue before it impacts the customer? [DET]	Risk priority number (RPN)

2. Place each risk (potential failure mode) on a single row in the potential issue column.

3. In the second column (severity), rate each potential issue using the following scale:
   - 10 = Complete loss, catastrophic impact to the customer
   - 9 = Critical impact to the customer
   - 3 = Major impact to the customer
   - 1 = Minor impact or nuisance

4. In the third column (likeliness of occurrence), rate each potential issue using the following scale:
   - 9 = This issue is likely to occur almost every time.
   - 7 = This issue occurs very frequently.
   - 3 = This issue occurs sometimes.
   - 1 = This issue rarely occurs or is not at all likely.

5. In the fourth column (detectability), rate each potential issue using the following scale:

- 9 = We only find out about this issue if the customer reports it to us.

- 3 = About 50% the time we catch this issue before the customer reports it to us.

- 1 = We know about this issue right away and almost always correct it before the customer is impacted in any way.

NOTE: Instead of detectability, you can evaluate the ease of diagnosing the problem, where

- 1 = It is an instant diagnosis.
- 3 = It requires a few questions or a few minutes to diagnose the problem accurately.
- 9 = The initial diagnosis is often incorrect, and a different problem is occurring than what was originally thought.

6. In the final column, multiply Severity x Occurrence x Detectability to calculate an overall RPN.

7. Sort in descending order by the RPN column to sort the potential issues in order by highest to lowest risk.

TOOL 4: CUSTOMER JOURNEY MAP
flexidian.com/customer-journey-map

The critical quick steps to create a journey map are:

1. Identify what customer persona(s) you are going to map.

2. Define the start and end point of the customer journey you plan to map. This, plus the identified persona(s), define the scope of your journey mapping effort. Make sure all your team members are aligned on the scope.

3. Create a list of all customer touchpoints within the customer journey that you have scoped.

4. For each touchpoint, identify whether it is initiated by the customer or internally (a reach to the customer).

5. For each touchpoint, list the purpose from the customer's perspective (what is the customer trying to achieve) as well as from the company's perspective (what is the organization trying to achieve).

6. Identify each touchpoint as "mandatory" (meaning *all* customers experience it) or "discretionary" (meaning it may be experienced by some customers).

7. Identify the method(s) of communication used at each touchpoint.

8. Identify your internal program, function, service, personnel, or other contact point with whom the customer is interacting at each touchpoint.

9. Notate the customer's emotion or level of satisfaction during each touchpoint.

10. Examine each touchpoint and document any lean wastes from a customer perspective.

11. Identify any areas of opportunity to improve the customer journey across the touchpoints.

12. Identify which touchpoints are "moments of truth"—interactions that are "make or break" for the customer.

13. Create an action register (see Tool 16) to address each pain point, waste, and opportunity. Prioritize moments of truth as highest-priority action items.

If the journey map is created internally without direct customer interaction, explore ways to involve customers in validating what you have mapped.

TOOL 5: KANO ANALYSIS
flexidian.com/kano-analysis

Apply the Kano model to your customer feedback survey results to identify improvement needs and opportunities.

1. Gather your customer survey results.

2. Create a table to sort your customer feedback:

Expected needs	Performance needs	Delighters

3. If you are using a scored survey, use these guidelines to sort your feedback into the listed categories:

   a. If you are using the 11-point NPS scale:

      i. Put the comments from your lowest detractors, 0–3 ratings, into the expected needs column.

      ii. Put the comments from your high detractors and passives, 4–8 ratings, into the performance needs column.

      iii. Put the comments from your promoters, 9–10 ratings, in the delighters column.

   b. If you are using a five-point or seven-point Likert scale:

      i. Put the comments from your bottom box respondents, into the expected needs column.

      ii. Put the comments in the middle ratings, 2–4 or 2–6, into the performance needs column.

      iii. Put the comments from your top box respondents, in the delighters column.

4. For the expected needs, identify any of these "must haves" that you are not currently delivering successfully. These must be addressed, and issues must be mitigated quickly.

5. For the performance needs, identify where there are improvement opportunities to deliver these more consistently or more effectively.

6. For the comments from delighters, take two approaches:

    a. First, look for ways to scale the delighter experience more broadly—what delighted this customer, and how can you deliver that experience to others?

    b. Second, look for suggestions for improvements. Often, someone who is delighted will still express an idea to impress them even further in the future. Acting on these will help you innovate for the future.

TOOL 6: FLEX HURDLES AND CLOCK DIAGRAM
flexidian.com/flex-hurdles-and-clock-diagram

1. On a blank sheet or whiteboard (physical or digital), draw a horizontal line down the middle. This line represents the hurdle bar.

2. As the facilitator, explain that items we place above the bar are "boosters," items that will help us achieve our purpose and leap over the hurdle, while items placed below the bar are "trip hazards," items that will trip us up, get in our way, and impact our success.

3. Ask participants to write their "boosters" and "trip hazards" in silence. If the group is physically together in a room, this can be most easily done by listing each individual item on a sticky note and placing the notes above/below the hurdle bar. It is often helpful to put all the boosters in one color and the trip hazards in another. If the exercise is being conducted virtually, participants can write their items directly onto the digital whiteboard space, above and below the hurdle line.

4. Once the idea generation in step 3 is completed, ask all the participants to silently read all the ideas across the hurdle field. Remaining silent, as a team, group like items together, forming affinity groups. The boosters and hurdles should still be on opposite sides of the hurdle bar at this point.

5. Next, look at the affinity groups and see what you can combine across the bar—what groups of trip hazards go with a group of boosters? Since you are now mixing together the positives and negatives, you can see why it was helpful in step 3 to use two different colors. The mixed group view of hurdle field at this point looks more like force-field analysis, where you can start to see the driving and restraining forces in juxtaposition.

6. Name each of the affinity groups (which now contain both boosters and trip hazards) to indicate the theme or commonality of each group.

7. Arrange the affinity group themes in a circle on a new whiteboard.

8. Beginning at the top of the circle (or clock) and proceeding in a clockwise direction, evaluate each pair of themes to decide which needs to be addressed first in your action planning. For each pair, draw an arrow with the arrowhead pointing toward the item that must be addressed first.

9. Continue doing this pairwise comparison until every theme has been compared with every other.

10. Count the number of arrowheads pointing toward each theme. This gives you a highest-to-lowest priority to address your themes through action planning.

TOOL 7: RESPONSE ROUTER
flexidian.com/response-router

1. Start with a list of the common issues or questions that face the team.

2. Create a table with the following headings:

Always "yes"	Negotiate	Always "no"	Reason	Alternatives

3. For each issue or question, if the answer is always "yes" (items that should always be approved), place them in the first column. If the answer is always "no" (items that should never be approved), place them in the always no column.

4. For those items that are always "no," indicate at least one reason in the reason column and suggest at least one alternative action in the alternatives column.

5. In the negotiate column, list:

   a. Items that require further discussion, fine-tuning, or escalation before they can be approved or resolved

   b. Anything new that is not already on the response router until a yes or no can be determined

6. As new issues arise, add them to the negotiate column until an answer is known and then move them to the yes or no.

7. Post the response router somewhere that can be easily accessed by all team members to ensure consistent issue handling.

TOOL 8: MILESTONE MAPPING
flexidian.com/milestone-mapping

The milestone map is a collection of the major deliverables of the work process being studied or redesigned. It is not usually used to map a current state process; rather, it is used to lay out a new workflow.

1. Agree with the team on the list of major steps and deliverables from start to finish of the scoped work.

2. Attach one piece of flip-chart paper to the wall for each milestone and label each at the top of the page.

3. For each agreed milestone, ask the project team this series of questions:

   a. Who is responsible for completing or executing this milestone?

   b. What exactly is the deliverable?

   c. When is the time frame that this deliverable is needed?

   d. Where will the work be done or sent?

   e. How does this deliverable need to be built, filed, executed, etc.?

   f. Who needs to be informed when this deliverable is complete?

4. As the facilitator, ask each team member to commit to the milestones as mapped.

5. Promptly document the results of this discussion and share the milestone map with all parties who need to know, including those in the meeting/workshop, as well as any additional stakeholders.

Milestone 1— Application
5W2H

Who? Developer/builder

What? *Complete* application

When? Need 30 days prior to economic development deadline

Where: Must send to city hall

How: Electronic filing is recommended

Whom to notify? Building department must be informed on EC-2

Milestone 2— Site Plan
5W2H

Who? Developer/builder

What? Finished plat submitted

When? Within 15 days after application is received

Where: Send to zoning

How: Electronic filing is required

Whom to notify? Building department must be informed on EC-2

Milestone 3— Plans Reviewed
5W2H

Who? Building department

What? Review to building code

When? Decision and documents needed within 21 days

Where: Leave at desk for pickup

How: Paper signature required

Whom to notify? Inform economic development on EC-2 spreadsheet

TOOL 9: FLEX 5S
flexidian.com/flex-5s

1. As the facilitator, explain that the 5Ss are five Japanese words that begin with the "s" sound. They have been translated into English words that also begin with "S" and that describe an approach to individual workspace discipline that will save time and effort every day.

2. Explain that an efficient workplace is one where everything is:

   Sorted — Determine which of your documents, tools, supplies, and references are necessary daily or most frequently vs. only for occasional use. Sort by importance as well as frequency of use.

   a. Determine which of your files, both physical and digital, are needed on a regular basis and which are saved for longer-term needs only (for example, audits, potential discovery, etc.).

   b. Take the same approach with your email. Which emails do you need readily on hand, and which messages are you saving for future reference only?

   Set in place — Always keep needed items in a location so you can find them quickly every time they are needed. Set your files in the place you need for ready access.

   c. In a digital environment, keep shortcuts or bookmarks to those files you use daily on your desktop in an organized location while storing those needed only occasionally in a file structure that does not clutter your desktop.

   d. When you open and edit documents, store them back where they belong. Do not create multiple versions in different locations.

   e. In a physical file environment, consider putting files that are not needed regularly into a storage area that is not in your regular workspace. Keep critical daily files close at hand.

   f. For email, keep only email demanding near-term action in your inbox. File all other notes into intuitive folder locations for future reference. As new email comes in, sort each note and set it in an appropriate location.

Serviceable—Your files and resources must be ready for use at all times.

g. Keep only the most current and up-to-date version of any documentation.

h. Implement a version control approach, especially for shared files. Make sure all stakeholders have ready access to the same "source of truth" and are not confused by outdated copies of files.

i. If multiple people need to access information about a customer, service incident, case, etc., make sure all relevant notes and pertinent information are stored together in an organized location—sticky notes on one person's desk aren't accessible broadly. Digital notes using a shared approach work better and keep the file more serviceable.

Standardized to make the first three Ss a recurring habit.

Sustained by making the approach a part of your employee onboarding, ongoing training, and incentive programs to bring up employees with 5S ingrained in the corporate culture.

TOOL 10: FLEX OEE—OVERALL
EMPLOYEE EFFECTIVENESS
flexidian.com/flex-o-e-e

1. For availability, define the measurement as: Actual work time/ Maximum available time

   Example: If someone is potentially able to work eight hours in a day but due to outside appointments, training time, etc. only actually works six hours in that day, their availability is simply 6/8 or 75%.

   While 100% availability is the theoretical maximum, the target for the team and/or individual should be set considering allowance for breaks, special projects, and other time away from work.

2. For efficiency, a few elements need to be defined:

   • Number of pieces produced—Think about the various types of work product a team or individual produces. These could be pieces of code from a computer program developer, reports produced, customer interactions completed in a contact center, etc.

   • Ideal processing time—Conduct an analysis of your average processing times for the same or similar work. Consider whether there are seasonal or time-of-day differences. What other factors may impact processing time? Set your ideal time based on your historical data to allow for expected variation.

   • Actual time—Use the same actual work time as in the equation above for availability.

   Example: A nurse practitioner sees eight patients in a day. Through record keeping, we see that a patient visit is ideally about 30 minutes. The nurse practitioner worked six hours that day. His efficiency was (30 minutes x 8 patients)/6 hours. Standardizing all the time elements to minutes for easier calculation, this becomes (30 x 8)/360 = 240/360 = 67%.

3. For quality, define what constitutes "right first time" vs. something needing rework? The calculation of quality is all good output divided by the total output (good and bad).

Example: A technician installs four air-conditioning units in a day. The next day, one of the customers calls to complain about a unit that is not working. The technician goes back on-site to make repairs. Her quality rating on installation of these four units was 75%.

4. Multiply Availability x Efficiency x Quality to calculate OEE.

5. Check for the six big losses: time fully out of work, downtime, reduced speed, delays, defects, and rework.

The OEE calculation gives an indication of the area of potential improvement.

TOOL 11: TABLE 1/TABLE 2
flexidian.com/table-1-table-2

For "instant triage" of incoming work:

1. Incoming work is opened by one person/team known as "Table 1."

2. Table 1 sorts all this work into two groups:

   a. Simple, which is work that can be accomplished with little effort

   b. Complex, which is work that will require investigation, contact with other people, or research to resolve

3. Table 1 gives all the complex work to the other team members, known as "Table 2," so they can begin the necessary research.

4. Table 1 begins resolving all the simple work until it is complete and then joins Table 2 to help with the complex work.

VARIATION: If the simple work in the office greatly outnumbers the complex, and if Table 1 is skilled enough to handle complex work:

Points 1 and 2 are the same as above, then:

3. Table 1 passes all the simple work to Table 2, so they can resolve those items quickly. When the simple work is complete, Table 2 assists Table 1 with the complex work.

4. Table 1 begins the research needed to resolve the complex work.

TOOL 12: CASI
flexidian.com/casi

The CASI chart is a two-axis diagram (below). The vertical axis is for expected quality and ranges from low expected quality at the bottom to high expected quality at the top. The horizontal axis is for level of effort that is required, also ranging from low to high.

Begin building the chart from the bottom right with the letter "I." This part of the graph is where expected quality is low, and the effort required to ensure quality is high. It is high because someone will be inspecting 100% of the output generated so any deficiency, defect, or failure is not missed before sending it to the customer.

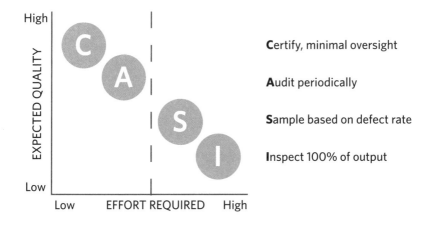

Certify, minimal oversight

Audit periodically

Sample based on defect rate

Inspect 100% of output

Count the number of times each type of problem arises. If you are looking at performance of individual team members, count the number of times a problem or error arises by team member.

Place the most commonly occurring errors and team members with the most problems at the "I" level. When someone is new or has had trouble with a particular type of task, the manager and the operator must both understand that 100% inspection will occur until performance improves.

When you see that the frequency of problems is decreasing relative to the other team members or relative to historic error rates, move that operator or issue to a sampling plan, "S," which can decrease over time as performance continues to improve, or which can be increased if quality begins to suffer.

Level three, "A," requires only periodic audit. When someone is able to be certified or an issue requires only minimal oversight, move them to "C" in the CASI model.

As team members progress from I to S to A to C, not only should they need less coaching, but they also should be held to increasing standards of quality.

Clearly defining which phase, which level of freedom, and which monitoring frequency each operator and issue requires at all times is critical.

TOOL 13: I-YOU-WHO
flexidian.com/i-you-who

Process documentation and work instructions should be written so clearly that a new hire could read and follow that document and be successful on the first day.

I-You-Who is a thorough list of the issues that an operator may encounter during a typical week.

1. Create a simple table with three columns:

I	YOU	WHO

2. In the first column, "I," list all items that the operator who owns this document must also own in action. In other words, the "I" is my responsibility. I am capable of doing it, I have the authority to do it, and it must be completed by me.

   "I" tasks generally reflect the operator's primary job description. They are the basic responsibilities that need to be carried out by the person serving in this role. Further, these "I" tasks must be handled by the operator and not sent to anybody else for action.

3. In the "you" category, list the tasks that must be routed to another person for action. They are either more complex, require a higher level of authority to execute, or carry some other reason for referring instead of executing them. The value of the "you" list is time savings in knowing exactly who handles each specific issue.

   It is advisable in the "you" section to list a primary and a backup for each item, if possible.

4. If an issue arises, and there is not a clear prescribed response, the "who" category is used.

5. Ensure each operator has a clear I-You-Who card that is updated/maintained regularly.

Once issues in the "who" section have been studied and a resolution is developed, move to the "you" section, and the operator will know who to consult for help. It may even become an "I" issue if the operator is armed with the tools necessary to resolve the issue the next time it arises. This evolution from "who" to "you" and eventually to "I" is the embodiment of empowerment for a workforce.

TOOL 14: HALF-LIFE FOLLOW-UP

1. If there is an action item that is scheduled for completion in 10 days, you as the facilitator will check with the owner of that task after five days. Check in with all action owners at the halfway point between when the action is assigned and when it is due.

   a. If the progress being made demonstrates that the action owner will successfully complete the item in time for the 10-day deadline, there is no further need to check on it.

   b. However, if progress is insufficient or unconvincing, you and the action owner review the item and its importance, and you reinforce the need to complete it on time.

2. Then, after cutting the original allotted time in half (due in 10 days = review in five days), you now check with the action owner again in half the remaining time (due in five more days = review again in about two days). If progress is still not certain, you will check again in another day.

By deploying a half-life project management approach, you keep the action item front of mind for the action owner and reduce the likelihood of reaching the due date without action being taken.

TOOL 15: FLEX RM
flexidian.com/flex-rm

Flex RM is a more concise version of an old, trusted waste reduction tool called the RAMMPP matrix. The "RM" in flex RM refers to reports and meetings, a subset of the targets from the older technique.

1. Ask the group to take a little time and list all the reports they generate. This list should include the reports that each individual creates and also a separate list of reports that two or more members of the group collaborate to build and share. The two lists should not include any repeated reports, but every report should also be listed only once on the full document.

2. Ask the group to list all the meetings they attend on a regular basis. This will often include weekly team meetings, daily huddles, project team meetings, update meetings, and more. Again, there will be two parts to the list: those meetings that each individual attends and a separate list for meetings where two or more members of the team participate. Each unique meeting should be listed only once when the list is complete. It can be very surprising to look at the long list of meetings once it has been built.

3. Begin at the top of this question list. If the answer is "No," then proceed through the remaining questions until the answer is "Yes."

   a. Can it (the report or the meeting) be eliminated? Can it be partially eliminated?

   b. Can it be done less often?

   c. Can it be delegated to somebody else?

   d. Can it be done using a more productive technology?

   e. Can it otherwise be simplified?

TOOL 16: ACTION REGISTER
flexidian.com/action-register

The action register lists the agreed-upon actions, owners, timeline, and next steps from which the project leader and process owners can manage and complete follow-up.

The facilitator brings the action register template into the meeting or workshop:

Agreed action	Primary owner	Action type	Next step	Due date of next step	Completion target
Short description of the improvement to be implemented	*Single person accountable to make sure the action is completed*	*Is it a quick win, project, etc. (see list below)*	*Describe the next thing to be done to make progress*	*Near-term date next step will be completed*	*Target date to complete all steps/final implementation*

In the action type column, the following options are suggested:

- **Quick win (or do it now)** — Something that can be achieved that day or very shortly after with a minimal number of steps by the owner. It does not require further approvals or discussion. The owner just needs to get it done.

- **Start a project** — Something that the team has approved/agreed to complete but will involve a more complex set of steps or interdependencies. The owner needs to draft and then work through a project plan to accomplish the desired end result.

- **Approval needed (or negotiate)** — Before moving forward, someone who was not in the meeting needs to approve the effort. The owner's next step is typically to gain the necessary approval. Once approved, the "type" column should then be updated to reflect quick win, start a project, etc.

- **Research (or study further)** — The team in the meeting did not have enough data to make a firm decision. More information is needed. The owner will look into it further and bring data back to the team to make a decision.

- **Consider for the future** — There may be actions the team would like to take, but timing is not right to pursue it currently for a variety of business reasons. It's good to track such actions and even assign an owner. The owner will be periodically reminded of the action and is responsible to bring it forward to the team for consideration again when the time is more ideal.

- **Do not pursue** — It may also be useful to track actions that were considered and rejected/decided against. For these, in place of a "next step," consider including a brief statement of why the decision not to pursue was made. If the decision factors change in the future, a "do not pursue" item might be more viable to consider. Additionally, it is sometimes helpful to report what the team decided not to pursue and why.

Draft the agreed action column during the meeting, capturing all the actions that need to take place.

At the end of the meeting, walk through the captured agreed actions, gain alignment from the meeting attendees, and complete the remaining columns.

Index

Note: Page numbers in *italics* indicate figures or tables. Page numbers followed by "n" indicate footnote.

About the Authors

Tracy Owens, CQE, CMQ/OE, is a process improvement consultant in Dublin, Ohio. He has been a Lean and Six Sigma practitioner since 1999 when he took on the role of Black Belt at the Kenworth Truck Company. From automotive manufacturing he ventured into supply chain logistics, insurance and finance, medical device manufacturing, legal and other professional settings, municipal governments, and many more working environments where process analysis, data analysis, and teamwork are required to drive lasting, positive changes. Since his time in the US Army in the early 1990s, Tracy has always believed in and demonstrated the importance of explaining clearly the objectives of the mission and not just directing or commanding specific tasks. There are two equally important components in influencing people: What you say, and how you say it.

In 2006, Tracy and a team of executives achieved call center certification by J.D. Power and Associates and it was during this period of time that the importance of group facilitation really crystalized as a multiplier for the effectiveness of improvement and change initiatives. He is author of two previous books from Quality Press: *Six Sigma Green Belt, Round 2* (2011) and *The Executive Guide to Innovation* (2013, co-author), and several articles in *Quality Progress* magazine. Tracy holds a masters degree in international business from Seattle University, and he was elected to the 2016 class of ASQ Fellows. Find Tracy on LinkedIn at: https://www.linkedin.com/in/tracyowensdublinohio

Therese Steiner, ASQ CSSBB, is the Director of Operational Effectiveness and Customer Experience at LexisNexis, where she has worked for 20+ years since completing her Juris Doctorate degree at the

University of Dayton School of Law in 1999. Therese is a 2020–2021 ASQ Board Member and Geographic Communities Council Region Director. Prior to these roles within ASQ, Therese served multiple terms as the ASQ Dayton Section Chair, where she led the Section to achieve PAR each year of her terms. She also continues to serve as the publication coordinator for the ASQ Service Quality Division. Therese has been a speaker on Customer Experience and Quality topics at global and regional conferences, including ASQ WCQI and OPEX World Summit, as well as at local meetings for ASQ and other organizations. In addition to her experience within ASQ, Therese is a Certified Customer Experience Professional, CCXP, with the Customer Experience Professional Association, CXPA. Within CXPA, Therese founded the Dayton/Cincinnati, Ohio, local CXPA network and has served multiple years as a network lead. Therese is a Business Process Management Professional, BPMP, through BPMInstitute. She leverages her Business Process Management expertise to implement robotic process automation, RPA, and business process management suite, BPMS, solutions that enhance internal efficiency and customer experiences at LexisNexis. Find Therese on LinkedIn at: https://www.linkedin.com/in/theresesteinerjd

WHY ASQ?

ASQ is a global community of people passionate about quality, who use the tools, their ideas and expertise to make our world work better. ASQ: The Global Voice of Quality.

FOR INDIVIDUALS

Advance your career to the next level of excellence.

ASQ offers you access to the tools, techniques and insights that can help distinguish an ordinary career from an extraordinary one.

FOR ORGANIZATIONS

Your culture of quality begins here.

ASQ organizational membership provides the invaluable resources you need to concentrate on product, service and experiential quality and continuous improvement for powerful top-line and bottom-line results.

www.asq.org/why-asq

ASQ
Excellence Through Quality